EYES ON NATURE®

DANGEROUS CREATURES

Kidsbooks®

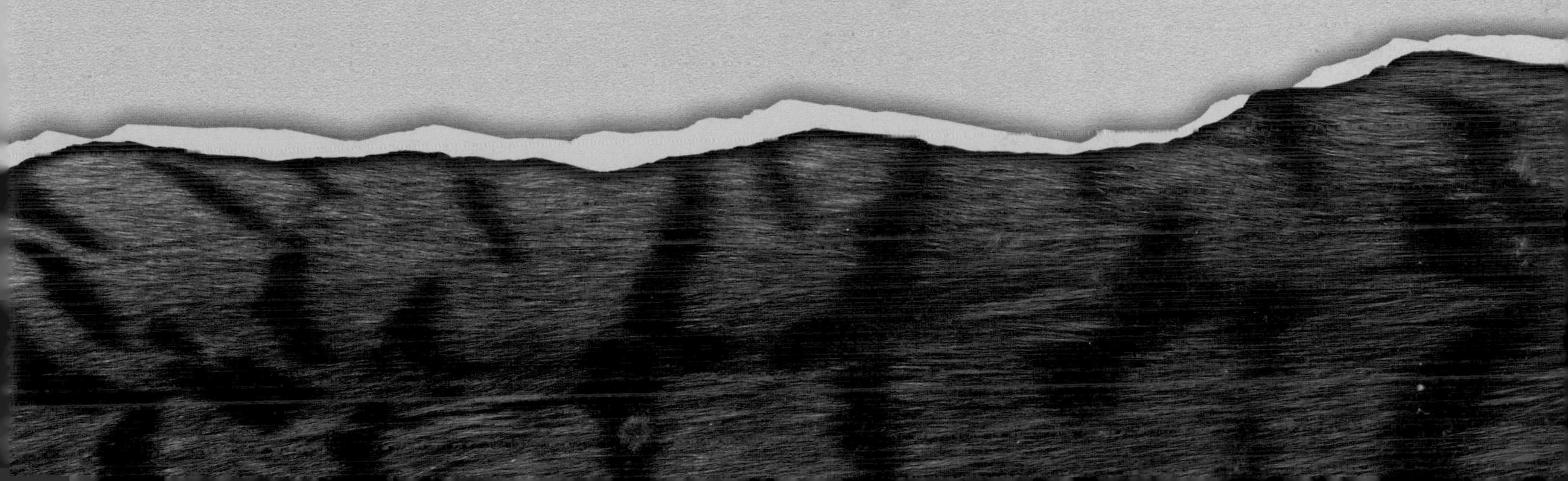

3535 West Peterson Avenue
Chicago, Il 60659

Printed in China

061002002GD

Table of Contents

Written by
Robert Matero
Rebecca Grambo
Jane P. Resnick
and
Donald Olson

Scientific Consultants

David Dickey
Dept. of Herpetology
American Museum of
Natural History

Edward M. Spevak
Wildlife Conservation
Society, Bronx Zoo

Merryl A. Kafka
New York Aquarium

Gary Brown
National Park Ranger
Bear-Management
Specialist

DEADLY SNAKES

Of the approximately 650 poisonous snakes, about 250 are dangerous to humans. When a poisonous snake bites, special glands pump venom through its hollow fangs and inject the poison into its victim.

◀ The muscular body of the rare, yellow eyelash viper helps it move easily through the dense tropical forest. Tree-dwelling snakes drink the moisture that collects on leaves.

PIT VIPER CLOSE-UP

Venomous Vipers

A viper keeps its extra-long fangs folded back against the roof of its mouth—until it's ready to strike. Vipers have wide heads in which they store their large venom glands. Gaboon vipers, found in tropical African forests, have the longest fangs—up to two inches—of any snake.

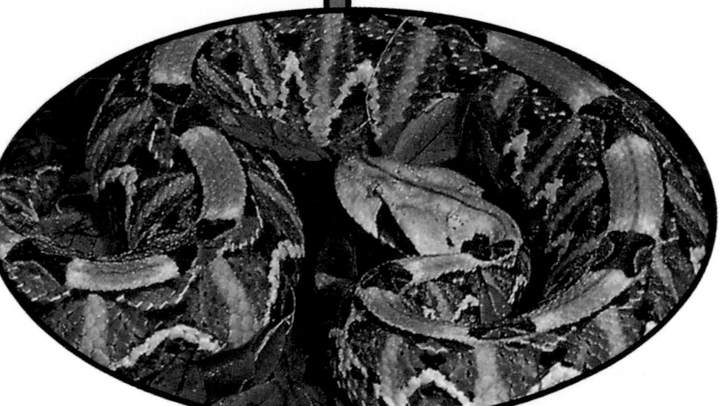

Gaboon Viper

Pit Vipers

Some vipers have pits — small holes—one on either side of their faces. These heat-sensing organs help the viper locate prey, especially at night.

▼ The best known pit viper is the rattlesnake. The rattle on the end of its tail is made up of dry, hard pieces of unshed skin. When shaken, the rattle makes a whirring, buzzing sound, warning strangers to stay away.

Copperhead ▲

The copperhead's markings allow it to blend in with the dead leaves on the forest floor. Although painful, this pit viper's bite is rarely fatal to humans.

Can you guess why I'm called a rhinoceros viper?

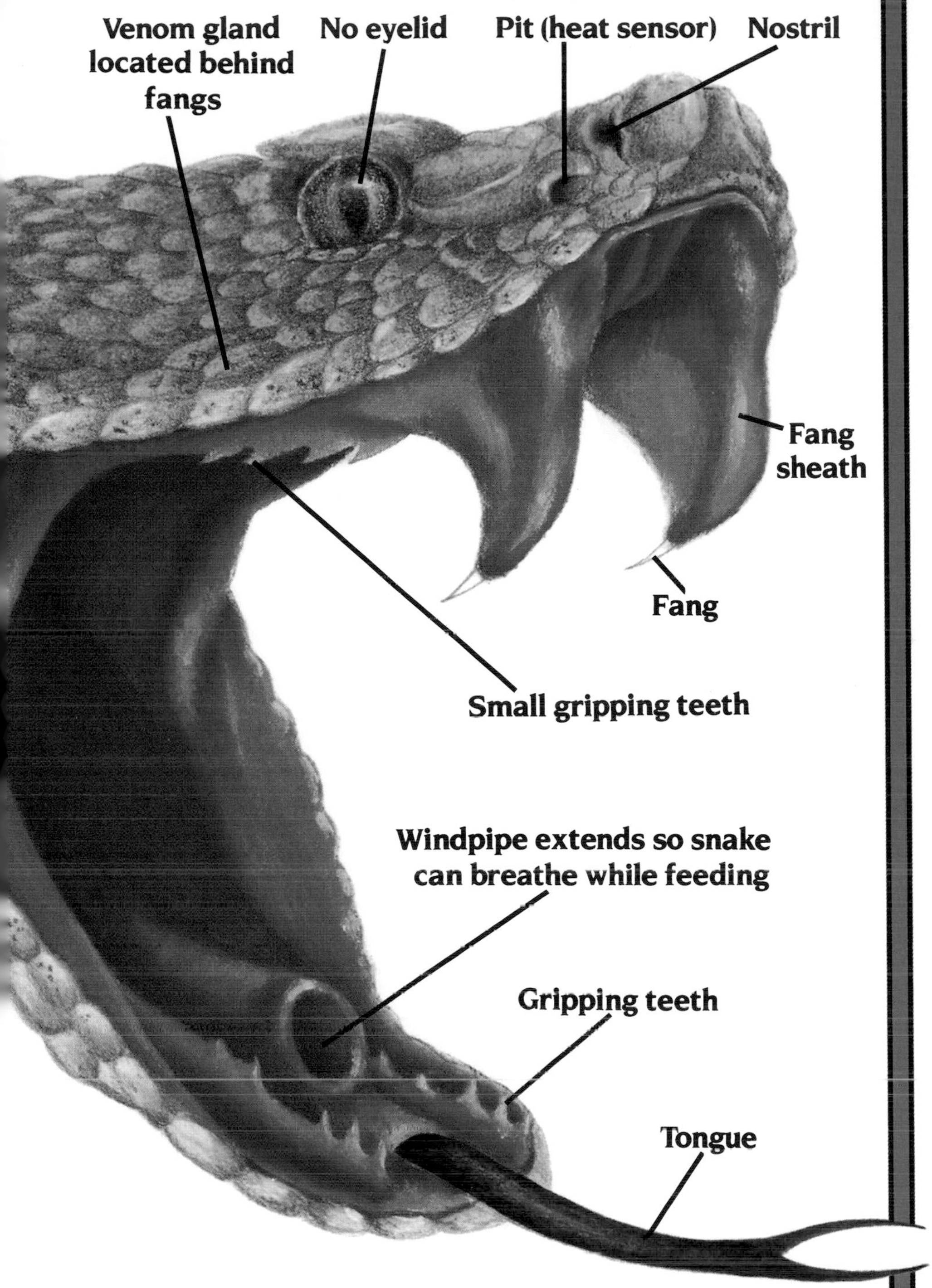

Venom gland located behind fangs

No eyelid

Pit (heat sensor)

Nostril

Fang sheath

Fang

Small gripping teeth

Windpipe extends so snake can breathe while feeding

Gripping teeth

Tongue

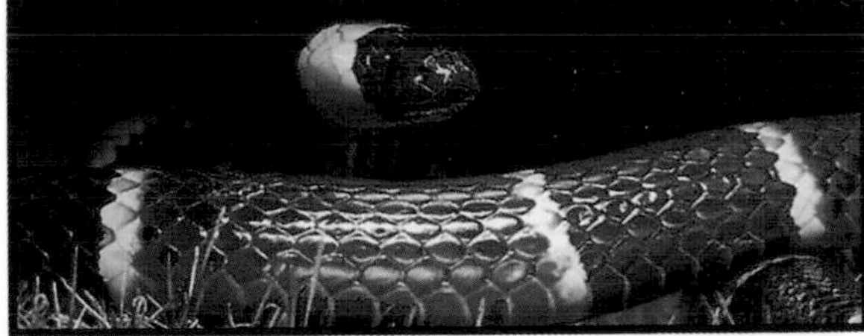

Coral Snake

Fixed Fangs

Unlike vipers, the colorful coral snake, along with its cobra, mamba, and sea snake relatives, has two short, sharp fangs fixed at the front end of its upper jaw.

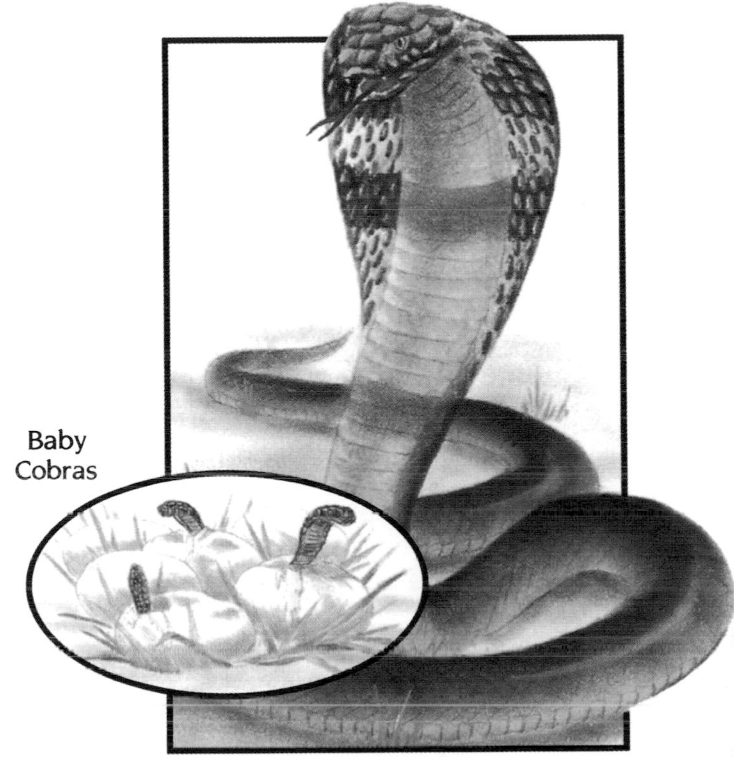

Hooded Terror ▲

The 18-foot king cobra is the longest poisonous snake in the world, with venom powerful enough to kill an elephant. When threatened, it spreads the loose skin on its neck into a "hood" several times wider than its body. Moving with its upper body raised off the ground, a hooded cobra is indeed a fearsome sight!

Aggressive baby cobras, armed with fangs and venom, will strike while still emerging from their shells.

Speed Demon ▶

The fast and deadly black mamba can move at a speed of seven miles per hour. It travels with one third of its 10 to 14 foot-long body lifted off the ground and can strike at the level of a person's head. Just two drops of venom from this African snake can kill a human in ten minutes!

DEADLY EMBRACE

Boas, pythons, and anacondas are constrictors—snakes that suffocate their prey. These types of snakes are non-poisonous. They capture their meals by suffocating their prey or simply biting and gripping them with their sharp teeth. After a large meal, a constrictor can go for many months without eating.

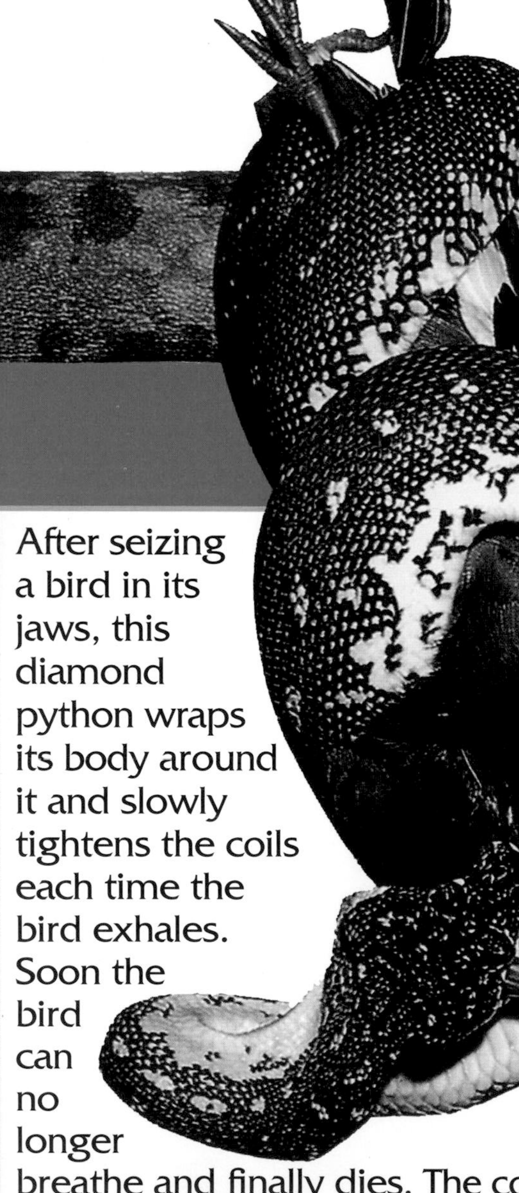

After seizing a bird in its jaws, this diamond python wraps its body around it and slowly tightens the coils each time the bird exhales. Soon the bird can no longer breathe and finally dies. The constrictor then swallows it whole, digesting everything except the feathers.

▼ These tree boas aren't having a conversation. They're just hanging out on their favorite branches. Heat sensors along their lips help them detect the tree-dwelling prey on which they feed.

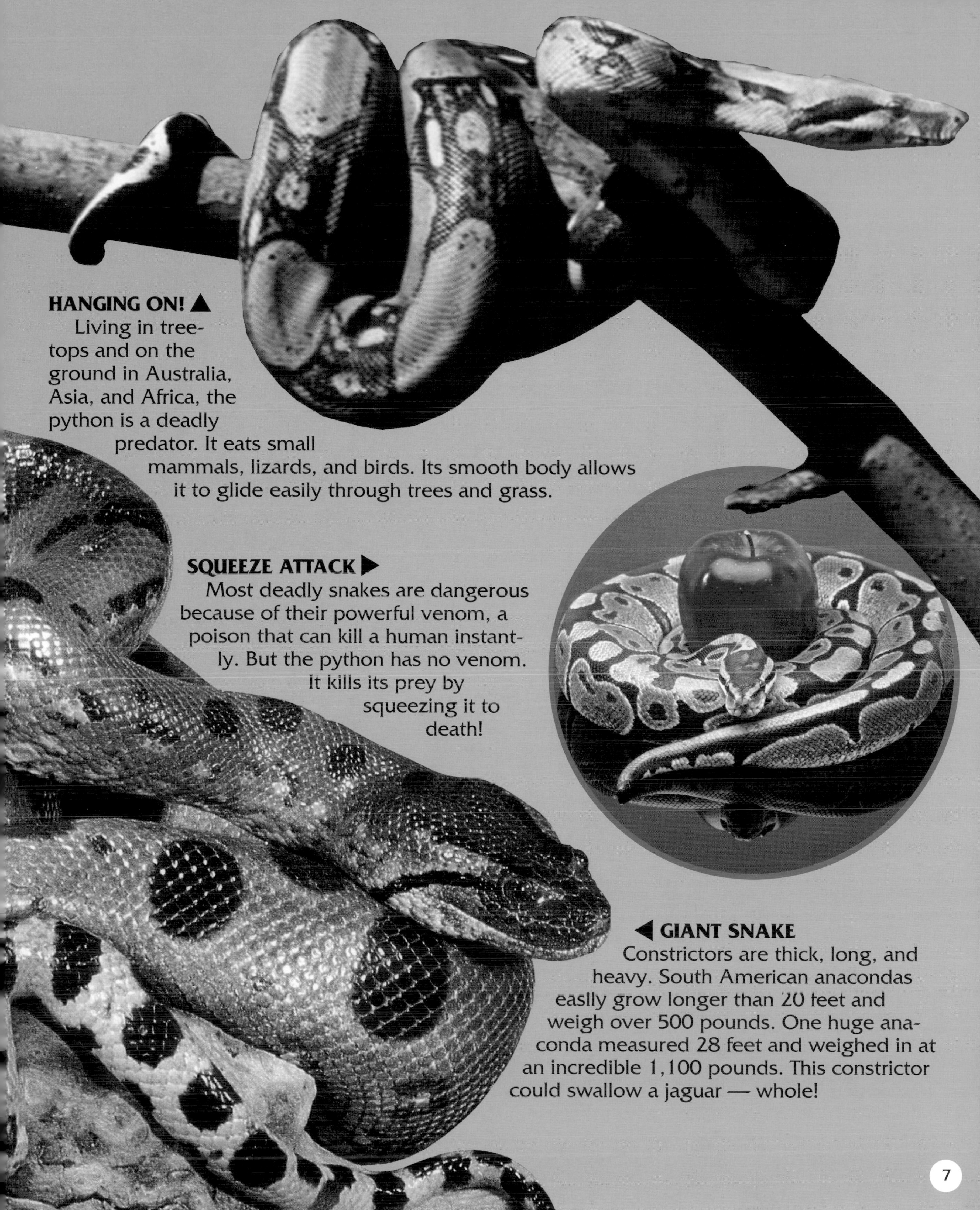

HANGING ON! ▲

Living in treetops and on the ground in Australia, Asia, and Africa, the python is a deadly predator. It eats small mammals, lizards, and birds. Its smooth body allows it to glide easily through trees and grass.

SQUEEZE ATTACK ▶

Most deadly snakes are dangerous because of their powerful venom, a poison that can kill a human instantly. But the python has no venom. It kills its prey by squeezing it to death!

◀ GIANT SNAKE

Constrictors are thick, long, and heavy. South American anacondas easily grow longer than 20 feet and weigh over 500 pounds. One huge anaconda measured 28 feet and weighed in at an incredible 1,100 pounds. This constrictor could swallow a jaguar — whole!

BIG DANGER

Animals use different tactics to hunt and for self defense. These animals use their claws, teeth, horns, tusks, and more to stay alive in the wild. If a human encountered any of these animals in an aggressive state, they'd have a slim chance of surviving.

▲ PROWLERS

Sleeping by day in caves or burrows, hyenas hunt by night, prowling in packs. Although well-known as scavengers, hyenas also hunt for live prey. They have extremely strong jaws and teeth which enable them to crack through bones of large animals. Although it will eat carrion (the remains of dead animals), it also likes to hunt for live prey. Working as a group allows hyenas to catch and kill large prey, such as zebras.

▲ KOMODO CLAWS

The Komodo dragon is the world's largest living lizard. It can grow up to 10 feet long. This reptile's long, forked tongue flicks in and out of its mouth, sensing both taste and smell. The Komodo dragon's powerful claws can cause serious damage during a fight with other lizards.

A hunting Komodo dragon bites its prey. If the bite does not kill right away, the infection from a Komodo dragon's drool will do so before long.

PACK HUNTING ▶

African wild dogs hunt in packs of up to 20 or more. Working together, they can bring down much bigger game than a single dog could.

CAPE ANGER

Surprisingly calm-looking in its appearance, the four-legged giant known as the Cape buffalo is actually quite dangerous. It eats mainly tall, coarse grass, but any encounters with humans can prove to be a threat. The sight or smell of a predator angers the Cape buffalo. It charges, unafraid, to protect its herd. Its great size and huge horns make for a very frightening sight! That is enough to scare off the most dangerous predators, even the lion.

TUSK DANGER

Both male and female African elephants grow tusks. These big front teeth can be over 11 feet long and weigh more than 200 pounds each, but most are smaller. An elephant also uses its tusks for self defense. Males will use their tusks for fighting for mates as well.

WIDE MOUTH

The hippo has sharp tusks that can grow to 28 inches in length. The hippo uses them to threaten attackers, and for fighting. He opens his mouth wide, revealing his tusks. If that is not enough to scare the challenger away, a fight follows—sometimes to the death.

WOLF!

Dangerous. If we know very little about wolves, this word seems to fit. But wolves are not dangerous to people. They are wild and fierce, like any other animal that hunts to feed itself. And, like all animals, they have their own way of life—separate from humans.

DOG YEARS

The wolf, as it is now, roamed Earth around one million years ago. Wolves *evolved*, or formed, from *carnivores* (meat-eaters) around 60 million years ago. The *canids* (which include wolves, dogs, and their relatives) separated from the *felids* (cats and their relatives) around 20 million years ago.

COLORFUL COAT ▶

Although known as the gray wolf, its coat is anything but plain gray. The variety of coat colors ranges from pure black to white, with shades of red, yellow, tan, silver, and brown in between. Any of these colors can occur within the very same family.

Red wolf ▲

◀ Gray wolves that live in the high arctic are called arctic wolves.

CANIS TIMES THREE

Scientists believed that there were two types of wolf—the gray wolf, *Canis lupis*, and the red wolf, *Canis rufus*. But recently, scientists have discovered a third type called the Ethiopian wolf, *Canis simensis*. The gray wolf lives in the northern hemisphere, and the red wolf lives only in the southeastern United States. The Ethiopian wolf is found only in Africa.

BIG?

"Big" is not exactly the right word for wolves. They vary in size. The average male weighs 95 pounds and the female, 10 pounds less. They stand $2^1/_2$ feet high and measure 5 to $6^1/_2$ feet from the tip of the nose to the end of the tail.

HELPFUL HUNTERS

Wolves live in the mountains, forests, and plains of the northern hemisphere. They have a special role in relation to their environment. It's called their *ecological niche* (pronounced NICH). Wolves are the most numerous of all predators that hunt large mammals in this territory.

REAL CHARACTERS

Like dogs, wolves are very intelligent animals and are capable of learning. Also, each one seems to have its own personality. Some are shy, while others are bold and outgoing. Some are very social within their group, while others hang back.

MEMBERS OF THE PACK

Wolves have a strong social nature. They live as a family, in what is called a *pack*. There is a pecking order within the pack, in which each wolf has a rank. Some wolves are *dominant*—aggressive and forceful. Others are *submissive*, giving in to authority.

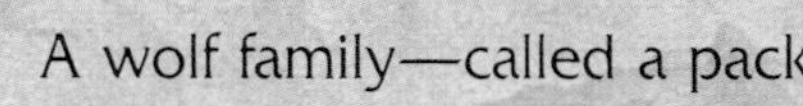

A wolf family—called a pack.

BLOOD TIES

A male and female head the wolf pack. They are the core of a group that is related by blood and affection. Other members are their offspring, ranging in age from pups to two or three years old. Most packs have six or seven members, although some may include as many as 15 wolves.

NUMERO UNO

The most powerful male wolf in a pack is known as the alpha (Alpha is the first letter in the Greek alphabet). His mate, the alpha female, helps rule the pack. They have forceful personalities, necessary for their dominant role. They make the decisions that affect the pack's survival.

FANG FIGHTS

Wolves within a pack rarely fight, because the alphas maintain order. However, wolves do fight members of other packs or intruding lone wolves. All wolf packs have a territory of their own. They patrol it and mark it, so that other wolves will know to stay out. If a strange wolf intrudes, it will be attacked and killed.

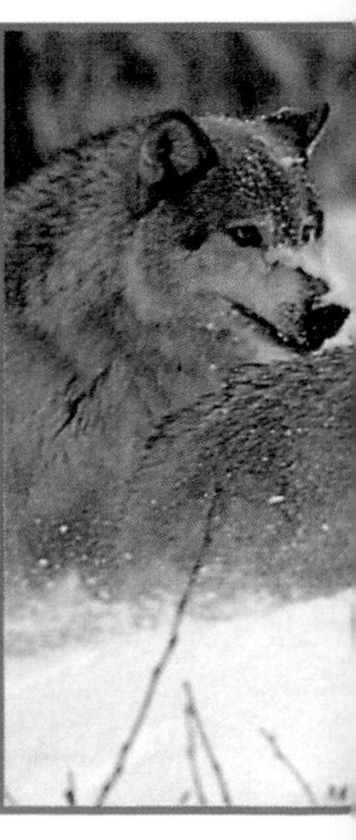

THE LONE WOLF

Do you know a "lone wolf," someone who stays apart? The expression comes from wolves who go off on their own. A pack grows and changes. Some young adults wait to move up to alpha positions when leaders become old or weak. Other wolves leave to wander and hunt alone, but they may start their own pack if they can find a lone mate.

OMEGA

In larger packs, there are wolves known as omegas (Omega is the last letter in the Greek alphabet). These wolves are picked on by all members of the pack. Sometimes they are bothered so much that they leave the pack.

An angry alpha tells an unwelcome intruder, "Get off my turf!"

PACK CONTROL

If two wolves are going to rule a pack, they have to be able to show their authority and keep the others in line. To do so, they constantly dominate the lower-ranking wolves, from the moment these wolves are born. The alpha male dominates the other males, and the alpha female keeps the other females in line.

▲(1)The alpha wolf growls at a lower-ranking wolf, who lowers his head.

KING PIN

Lower-ranking wolves (subordinates) are constantly disciplined by alphas. Alphas growl, bite, chase, and even pin them to the ground while the rest of the pack looks on (1-4).

(2)The alpha bites and tackles ▲ the subordinate.

(3)The alpha pins the ▶ subordinate.

TOP TAIL

A wolf's tail is like a flag waving its rank. Alphas hold theirs high. Wolves below the alphas keep their tails low. And lowest-ranking members tuck their tails between their legs.

▲This male alpha wolf is holding his tail high.

▲With her tail tucked between her legs, this subordinate female slinks off.

STERN STARE

A stern, unwavering stare from an alpha wolf is enough to convince members of the pack to bend to his or her authority. Submissive wolves will pull their lips back in a defensive grin, lower themselves to the ground, and, if they can, turn and slink away. Sometimes they roll on their backs to make things very clear that they know who's boss.

YOU'RE THE BOSS

Lower-ranking members show respect and affection for the alpha wolf in a special greeting ceremony. They approach him or her with their bodies low, fur and ears flattened. Then, reaching up, they lick and nip the alpha's face affectionately.

(4)Finally, the lower-ranking wolf begs forgiveness. ▼

WOLF TALK

Wolves are among the most loyal of animals, having deep attachments to their companions. Through gestures and body movements, wolves communicate their feelings. This "wolf talk" keeps the pack together and working as a group.

Affection between wolves is shown by nuzzling, licking, and cuddling.

BEGGING FOR BITES

The alpha wolves are usually at the head of the pack when attacking prey. They are the first ones to take bites out of the kill and get the choicest parts to eat. Lower-ranking wolves have to beg for food. They lay their ears back and, with their mouth closed, whine and paw at the alpha's face. Every now and then, they manage to grab some food.

PALS THAT HOWL

To people, the howl of the wolf is the sound of the wild. To wolves, it may be a party. Wolves most often howl as a pack—to encourage their closeness, to celebrate a successful hunt, to find separated members, and to tell other packs to keep back. On a calm night, howling can broadcast 120 square miles.

Alpha wolves make it clear to others that they should wait their turn to eat.

TELLTALE TAIL

A wolf also uses its tail to express how it's feeling. A tail raised and slightly curving up at the tip means the wolf is sure of itself. If the tail is dropped but curved up at the end, the wolf is being friendly. If the tail is between the wolf's legs, the wolf is being friendly or is afraid.

FACE TO FACE

Wolves have very expressive faces. A fearful wolf flattens its ears and covers its teeth in a meek smile. An angry wolf bares its teeth and points its ears forward. A wolf that is threatened and afraid keeps its ears back but also bares its teeth, letting its tongue roll out. These are clear messages, and pack mates know how to react to keep the peace.

This wolf is being threatened and is afraid.

One wolf sits down to show the other that he doesn't want to fight.

BUILT FOR HUNTING

At this very moment wolves are hunting. They are physically built to do so. If there is snow, they are leaving a neat line of single tracks, hind feet following exactly behind front feet. This gait occurs because a wolf's legs are spaced very close together. It is an advantage in deep snow and difficult country.

TEETH FOR TOOLS

Teeth are weapons, and wolves have an arsenal of forty-two. Four pointed canines curve out near the front of the jaw, two on top and two on bottom. With these two-inch spikes, a wolf can pierce through tough hides and thick hair and hang on. With their *carnassials*, or molars, adult wolves can crush the thigh bone of a moose.

ON THEIR TOES

When wolves hunt, they are swift and silent—because they run on their toes. Like horses and cats, wolves keep the back parts of their feet raised when walking or running. Moving in such a way, with strong, muscular legs, wolves have long strides. They can trot for long periods at five miles an hour and race up to 40 miles an hour.

RADAR EARS

Hearing is a hunting skill, and wolves have the best. Wolves listen by turning their ears from side to side. By recognizing where the sound is loudest, they can tell the direction the noise is coming from, Ears up, they can hear sounds several miles away.

WOLF PARKA

In order to hunt in winter, wolves are protected by a fur coat as thick as three inches. Nearest to the wolf's flesh is a dense woolly undercoat to keep it warm. Black-tipped guard hairs form a longer, rougher outercoat that shuts out moisture and sheds water. In this fur-lined raincoat, a wolf can go anywhere.

This wolf knows how to follow its nose.

THE NOSE KNOWS

Noses to the air, wolves pick up the scent of prey before they detect it in any other way. If the wind is blowing from the direction of the hunted animal, they can catch the odor as much as a mile and a half away—before they hear or see their prey. Noses down, wolves can also follow fresh tracks with their sharp sense of smell.

PACK HUNTERS

Wolves are carnivores (meat-eaters). They are predators that hunt in groups. Sometimes a small animal like a beaver, rabbit, mouse, or bird is a mouthful for a single, hungry wolf. But in order to feed its many members, a pack must kill large prey, such as deer, caribou, elk, moose, or mountain sheep.

DELICATE BALANCE

Wolves are part of nature's scheme. Generally, they kill the old, sick, and young of their prey.

Often, the group on which they prey benefits as well. If the sick die, there is less chance of disease spreading. If older animals are killed, there is more food for the young. This "balance of nature" helps keep predator and prey healthy.

GETAWAY PREY

Fierce as wolves may seem, most of their prey escapes. Less than 10% of wolf hunting is successful. In one three-day study, wolves pursued 131 moose but killed only six. What happens? Deer and caribou can outrun wolves. Moose may fight back. That's 1200 pounds of animal with sharp antlers and heavy hooves—enough to crush a wolf's skull.

Usually, bison will defend themselves by grouping and greeting wolves head-on, with weight and horns. Wolves then try to separate one from the herd.

CLEAN PLATE

Food is life, but food is scarce for many wolves. Wolves can survive for two weeks without eating—and gorge themselves when they do. (An adult wolf can eat as much as 20 pounds at one time). Bolting down the flesh of its kill in large pieces, a pack of wolves leaves nothing behind—only the hooves and largest bones.

◀ A wolf is marking its territory.

WE ARE HERE. DON'T INTERFERE.

Survival depends on hunting grounds, and wolves will fight to defend them. A pack's territory ranges from 30 square miles to 800 square miles, depending on the kind of animal they hunt. Borders are posted with scent markings—urine sprayed on tree stumps and rocks—and advertised with group howling.

BURIED TREASURE ▲

Sometimes wolves will store some of their kill by dropping it in a hole and covering it over. Later, when hunting is difficult, they go back to this cache (sounds like "cash") and dig up their buried treasure.

COYOTE COUNTRY

Although they live only in North America, coyotes are found from Alaska to Costa Rica, throughout Canada, and from the Pacific coast to the Atlantic. They live in Death Valley, California, where the temperature soars to 135°F, and on the plains of Canada, where it drops to -65°F. Today, there are more coyotes than ever before.

IN GOOD VOICE

Coyotes are musical. Their voices have a high and low range. Their howling is very close to singing, with a variety of sounds—barks, huffs, yelps, woofs, and yaps. They recognize each other's voices. When one coyote begins howling, others within hearing distance join in. Mated coyotes keep in touch through howling when separated. They even have a greeting song.

UP TO SIZE

The average coyote is two feet high, four feet long (including its tail), and looks like a medium-sized dog, similar to a German shepherd. Twenty-five pounds is the average weight, although some are as heavy as 70 pounds. Whatever the size, thick fur makes coyotes look larger than they are.

COYOTE COUPLES

Coyotes are social animals that live in family groups. A male and female mate for life or, at least, may stay together for several years. They become much closer in the month before breeding. They hunt together, sing howling duets, and show affection by pawing and nuzzling.

A coyote raiding a chicken coop.

BUILT JUST RIGHT

Coyotes have the tools to be excellent hunters. With their powerful legs, they can leap up to 14 feet. With keen eyesight, they can see the slightest movement yards away. With their sharp hearing, they can detect the faintest stirrings of mice under the snow. And with a strong sense of smell, they can pick up a human scent and run away to safety.

CAMOUFLAGE COAT

Coyotes have coats that keep them undercover, so they can sneak up on prey and hide from predators. The ones that live in wooded regions have dark fur, which makes them difficult to see in the underbrush. Desert-dwelling coyotes have tawny coats that blend in with sand and weathered rock.

DANGEROUS SHARKS

Here's the nightmare: You see a fin and then a giant shark grabs you and crushes you with its teeth. Wake up! It's probably a dream. Here are the facts. Worldwide, fewer than 100 people are attacked in an average year by sharks. Some of these cases are provoked attacks, where the shark is caught, trapped, speared, or somehow bothered by people.

The great white is one of the most dangerous sharks!

THE GREATEST

The great white shark is one of the largest, most deadly predators. Credited with more attacks on humans than any other shark, it can grow up to 11 1/2 feet long and weigh up to 3,000 pounds. Twenty-foot great whites have also been reported! It's one of the few sharks known to lift its head above water.

TIGER OF THE SEA

The tiger shark is second only to the great white in the number of attacks on people. There is very little in the sea that the tiger shark doesn't eat. Some have been found with a few weird objects in their bellies—such as boat cushions, unopened cans of salmon, an alarm clock, tar paper, and a keg of nails! ▶

The great hammerhead is sometimes found in water only 3-feet deep.

Mako shark

HAMMER HORROR

Seeing a hammerhead in the water might be enough to scare a swimmer to death, but scientists don't think that hammerheads are man-eaters. However, they consider a few kinds, like the great hammerhead and the smooth hammerhead, to be potentially dangerous because of their size.

KNACK FOR ATTACK

About 27 kinds of sharks are known to have attacked humans, and there are others considered dangerous. Shark attacks usually occur where there are a lot of people—in fairly warm, waist-deep water. It's possible that all the vibrations in the water resemble those of a wounded fish—a favorite shark meal. Attacks also occur where people are fishing.

◀ The blacktip reef shark is dangerous.

Tiger shark

SWORD SWALLOWER

The mako is powerful and thought to be dangerous. It is the fastest shark of all, clocked at 43 miles per hour. It is known to leap out of water—sometimes into boats! Also, the mako seems to have very little fear. A large, 730-pound mako was once caught with a 120-pound swordfish in its stomach—sword and all!

Bull shark

▲ BRUTAL BULL

The bull shark doesn't look as frightening as the great white, but it is in some ways more dangerous—certainly in the tropics. Listed as the third-most dangerous man-eater, the bull shark swims in places that people do—in salt water and fresh water.

NO-TEAR WEAR

People have tried over and over again to come up with chemical products and special diving suits that will repel sharks. One kind of suit found to help protect divers against bites is made of steel mesh.

A diver wearing a steel-mesh suit while feeding a shark.

PHYSICAL SHARK

Sharks are one of the most dangerous creatures in the wild. Their physical traits and keen sense of smell, sight, hearing and taste all contribute to how they hunt and why they are feared from sea creatures and humans.

NEVER-ENDING TEETH ▼

Sharks have an endless supply of teeth, which are set in soft tissues. A shark may grow and use over 20,000 teeth in a lifetime. Each time a shark loses a tooth, another one comes forward and takes it place. Typically a shark has three working rows of teeth with 25 teeth in each row.

◀ SHARK FIN

The dorsal fin is located on a shark's back. Its main purpose is to stabilize the shark against rolling and assist in sudden turns. The sight of an approaching dorsal fin signals that it's time for prey to steer clear.

◀ TIGER TAIL

The larger upper lobe on the top of the tiger shark's tail helps deliver the maximum amount of power when sudden bursts of speed are needed. This enables the shark to easily twist and turn when on the hunt.

DON'T TREAD ON ME! ▼

Slow-moving nurse sharks are normally harmless to humans. If a diver steps on or bothers one of these huge bottom dwellers, he will be faced with a strong jaw and thousands of small serrated teeth. And the nurse shark *will* bite.

EYE SPY A SHARK! ▲

Most sharks have strong night vision. Their eyes have a mirror-like layer that reflects light. Sharks have eyelids, but they do not blink because the surrounding water cleans their eyes. Some sharks like the great white shark roll their eyes backwards to protect themselves when attacking prey.

◀ ELECTRICAL WAVES

Sharks generally rely on their advanced sense of smell to find prey. Another sense that sharks use when they are in closer range of their prey is lateral lines, an organ that runs along the sides of their body. Lateral lines are used to sense movement and vibration in the surrounding water.

CROCODILIANS

Alligators, crocodiles, gharials, and caimans belong to a group of reptiles known as crocodilians. They lived alongside the dinosaurs, but unlike them, crocodilians were able to adapt to the Earth's changes and survive.

Members of the crocodile family have long, sleek bodies covered with hard, bony scales that keep them well protected. They never stop growing and are thought by some to be the smartest of all reptiles.

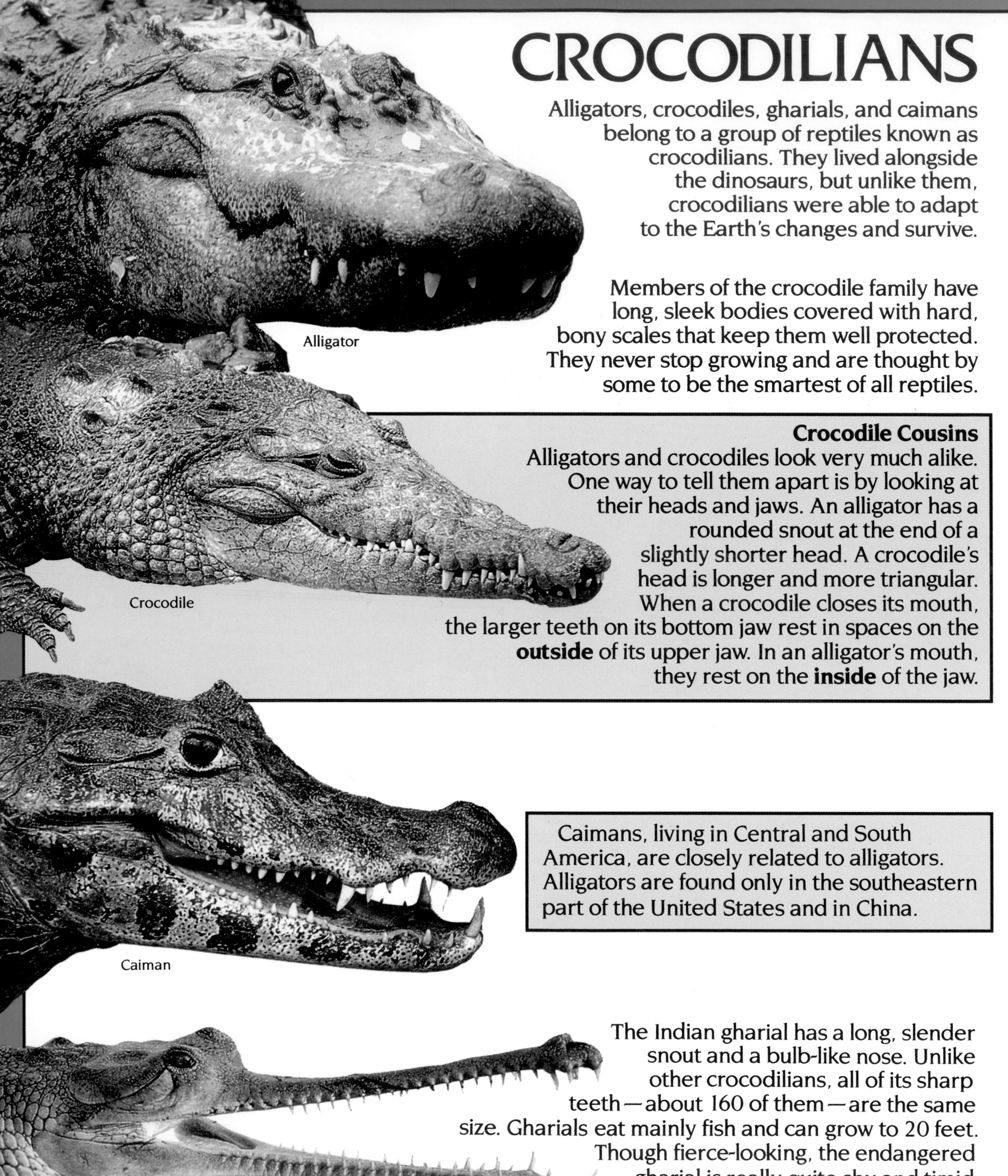

Alligator

Crocodile

Caiman

Gharial

Crocodile Cousins
Alligators and crocodiles look very much alike. One way to tell them apart is by looking at their heads and jaws. An alligator has a rounded snout at the end of a slightly shorter head. A crocodile's head is longer and more triangular. When a crocodile closes its mouth, the larger teeth on its bottom jaw rest in spaces on the **outside** of its upper jaw. In an alligator's mouth, they rest on the **inside** of the jaw.

Caimans, living in Central and South America, are closely related to alligators. Alligators are found only in the southeastern part of the United States and in China.

The Indian gharial has a long, slender snout and a bulb-like nose. Unlike other crocodilians, all of its sharp teeth—about 160 of them—are the same size. Gharials eat mainly fish and can grow to 20 feet. Though fierce-looking, the endangered gharial is really quite shy and timid.

A Watery Life

Crocodilians are built for a life in and around water. They are strong swimmers — wiggling through the water with their powerful tails propelling them forward. When floating, the eyes, ears, and nostrils, positioned higher than the rest of the head, are exposed above the water. But when underwater, where they can remain for over an hour, transparent shields slide across their eyes to protect them.

Saltwater Crocodile

Beware That Smile

Silently gliding forward, eyes steady and riveted, the crocodile is a fearsome and aggressive hunter. It will attack large animals and is very dangerous to humans. Alligators,on the other hand, are shy. They will bite if disturbed but most likely will swim or run away when approached.

Record Breakers

Adult male crocodiles measuring over 14 feet are not uncommon, but the all-time champions of size are the saltwater crocodiles of southeast Asia which sometimes stretch out to more than 20 feet.

This crocodile enjoys a peaceful float, but don't be fooled… he's got an eye out for any intruders.

Underwater Dining

Crocodilians cannot chew their food—they swallow it whole. If their prey is too large, they grab it with their sharp teeth, drag it underwater until it drowns, then rip it into chunks with powerful twists of their bodies. A throat flap keeps the water out of their lungs when diving, so they can swallow their food underwater.

A crocodile continually grows new sets of teeth to replace the ones lost while hunting. It can go through about fifty sets in a lifetime!

Powerful Jaws

With one snap an alligator's jaws are powerful enough to cut a large animal in two. However, the muscles which open its mouth are so weak that once shut the alligator's mouth can easily be held together.

All crocodilians are flesh eaters and feed on any animals they can catch — from birds and fish to zebras or antelope. Gharials eat mainly fish. Some crocodilians swallow small stones which help to grind their food and also enable them to float low in the water.

Lazy Day ▶

Much of this crocodile's day is spent basking in the warm sun. At dusk it will perk up and begin hunting for its dinner.

Alligator Nest

Nests and Babies

Female crocodiles dig a hole into which they deposit their eggs in two or three layers before covering them with sand. Alligators prepare rounded nests of mud and decaying vegetation above the ground. Both nests protect the eggs as the sun's warmth incubates them. Unlike most other reptiles, crocodilian mothers guard their nests and stay close to their babies after they are born.

This crocodile is not eating her eggs. Her babies are ready to be born and she's gently rubbing the shells so that they may be released.

Squeak! A saltwater crocodile, 12 inches long and weighing five ounces, emerges from its shell. As an adult it can measure 20 feet and weigh as much as 2,000 pounds.

A mother alligator carries her babies to the water on her back—sometimes in her mouth—as carefully as a mother dog carries her puppies. The hatchlings are miniature versions of their parents.

POISON ARROW FROGS

The poison arrow frog (also called the poison dart frog) is a brightly colored, tiny amphibian that lives in the rain forests of Central and South America. No more than 1 inch long, this little frog's skin can be green, blue, red, yellow, or orange. Although beautiful, this skin is also this frog's best means of defense.

POISON ATTACK ▲

If a predator licks a poison arrow frog, they will get very sick, very quickly, and will never attack again. The poison enters the predator's bloodstream and affects nerves and muscles. Sometimes, just one lick can be fatal!

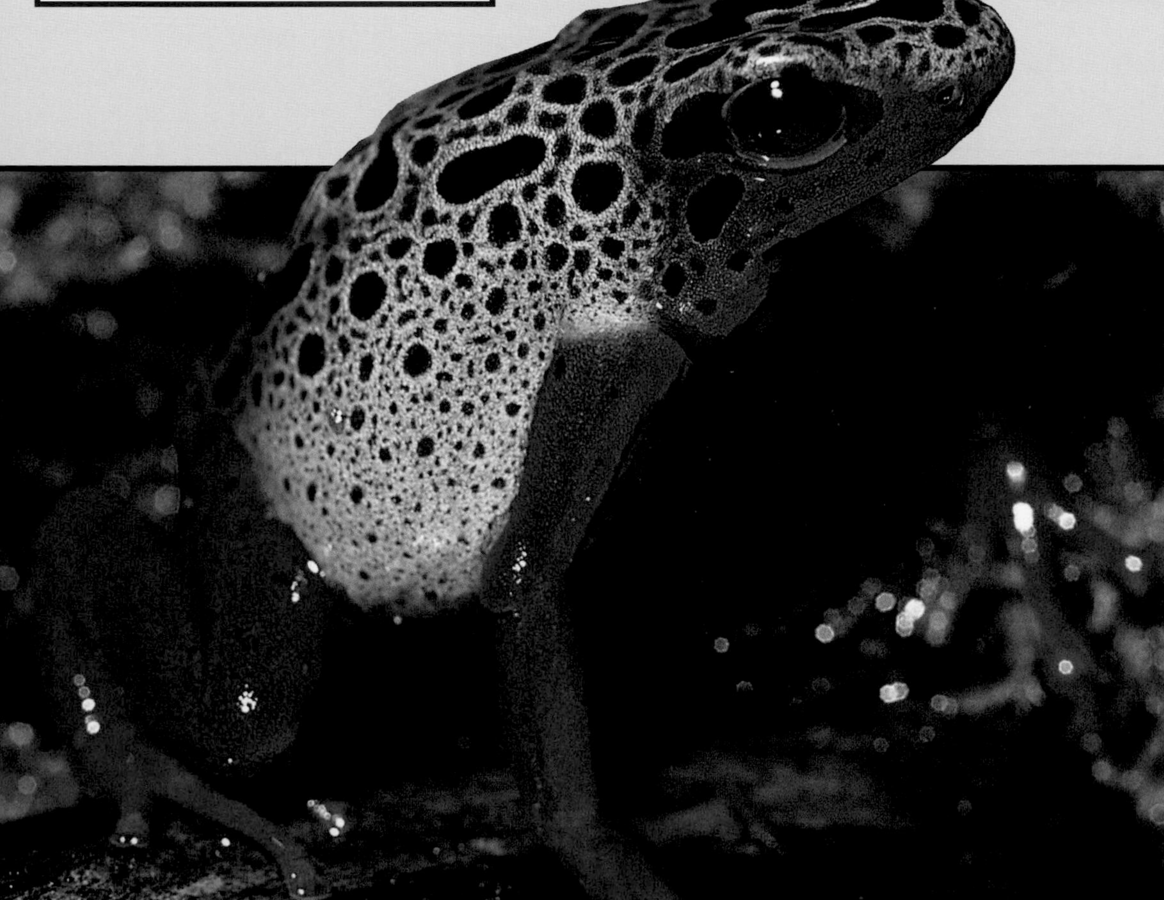

◀ MUCUS DEFENSE

The skin of a poison arrow frog is covered in mucus. This helps the frog stay moist when it's away from water. It also helps its tadpoles (babies) stay attached to the mother. However, the mucus also contains one of the most powerful poisons in the world! This poison has to be strong because many of the poison arrow frog's predators, such as snakes and spiders, are not harmed by weaker poisons.

◀ LIGHT EYES

Unlike other frogs, poison arrow frogs are more active during the day. They sleep at night which is the opposite of other frog species.

HUNTING SKILLS ▼

Native people in South America apply the poison that comes from the skin of these frogs to darts and arrowheads for hunting small animals.

LOVING PARENTS ▲

The poison arrow frog carries its young to a nearby pool when the tadpoles are grown and ready to swim. When the parents and tadpoles reach the top of the rainforest trees, the parents let go of their young in the pools of water that form in certain plants.

FROG MEDICINE ▼

Long used by Ecuadorian Choco Indians as a weapon, the venom from the poison arrow frog can help as well as hurt. One compound in the venom acts as a painkiller that is 200 times better at fighting pain than is morphine, a drug used in hospitals.

WILD CATS

Domestic Burmese kitten

There are about three dozen different species of cats, all in the family Felidae. They are diverse in size, from a ten-foot, 600-pound tiger, to the smallest domestic house cat weighing only a few pounds. But all cats (felines) share many of the same characteristics.

Cats are grouped into categories: big cats—the lion, tiger, leopard, and jaguar; and small cats, which include cats in the full range of sizes. The difference between the two is not size but sound—the big cats can roar, the small cannot.

POUNCING PREDATOR

Jaguar

The cat is a jumping, leaping creature able to land on its feet and pinpoint its landing. With lightning quick reflexes, agility, and strength, cats balance in risky places, recover from falls, and spring off the ground. As a leaping, pouncing predator the jaguar is deadly accurate.

COATS OF COLOR

The colors and markings of the cat are its glory. Every coat is individual. The black stripes of the tiger are his own. The spots of the cheetah, leopard, and jaguar are all different. Most coats match their surroundings so that the stealthy, hunting cat will not be heard *or* seen.

Cheetah

NAME THAT CAT

Cats have wonderful names like jaguar, puma, ocelot, cheetah, and lynx. Many of the names were given by people who respected and feared the fierce cats that lived among them. Jaguar comes from the South American Indian name *yaguara*, which means “a beast that kills its prey with one bound.”

Cougar

African wild cat

THE BEAUTIFUL BEAST

All cats are carnivores, meat-eaters who hunt for their food. Their bodies are like well-oiled machines with flexible skeletons, strong muscles, excellent eyesight, keen hearing, powerful jaws, and vicious teeth. They are the nearest thing to a perfect stalking, hunting animal in the world. Because of their beauty, secretiveness, and fierceness, cats have always been a symbol of mystery and power to man.

HOUSE CAT HISTORY

The sociable domestic cat is the favorite pet of millions of people. Descended from the African wild cat, cats began living with humans in Egypt about 4,000 years ago. They were so valued that the Egyptians considered them sacred and worshipped them in the form of a goddess that had the head of a cat.

The marvel of the house cat is its double nature. A delightful, tame companion, the cat still has the body of a hunter and carries a touch of the wild wherever it lives.

FELINE FEATURES

The physical ways of cats are fascinating. No one trait in itself, but a combination of characteristics, enables cats to feed, communicate, and live successfully in many different habitats.

CLEAN MACHINE

Cats groom or clean themselves, and each other, with a built-in scrub brush, a tongue rough as sandpaper. A cat's tongue is covered with tiny, hard spikes—perfect for picking up loose dirt or hair, or rasping the last shreds of meat off a bone.

UNDERCOVER ▲

A cat is a warm-blooded animal with a double-layered fur coat that protects it from wet and cold. The outer layer is made up of long, coarse hairs called guard hairs. The under fur, close to the body, is soft and downy. The thick fur of the two snow leopards shown above enables these cats to live on the cold Himalaya Mountains of Asia.

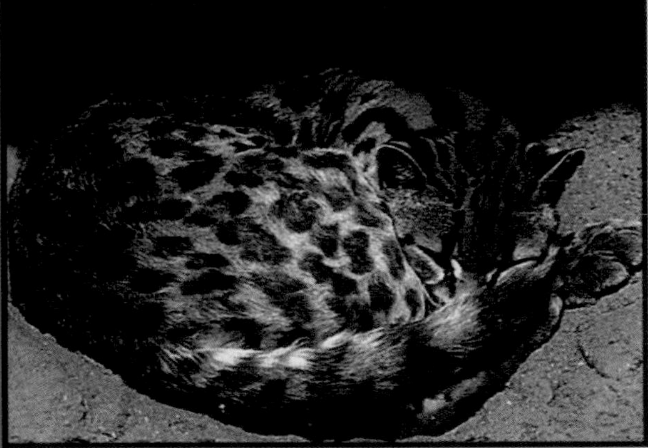

SLEEPYHEAD

Catnap is a word invented to describe the way cats sleep—for short periods of time. This ocelot, like all cats, sleeps *often*—about twice as much as other animals.

EAR FULL

Cats, masters of silence in their own movements, are quick to hear the noises that others make. With funnel-shaped outer ears and a keen sense of hearing, cats can pick up sounds that are too faint or too high for humans to hear.

African caracal

TOUGH TALK ▲

Cats have their own communication system: hissing, spitting, growling, and snarling. Purring, the perfect sound of contentment, is for pleasure.

WHISKER WAYS ▶

A cat's whiskers are not just cute. They are organs of touch almost as sensitive as fingertips. They help a cat avoid objects, judge spaces, and feel its way in the dark.

◀ MINE!

A cat is a territorial creature. It will scratch trees and spray urine to mark its property, so that other cats will keep off. A domestic cat has more civilized ways of marking. It may rub the furniture or a person's legs with the scent glands on its head or at the base of its tail.

BUILT TO KILL

To be a cat is to be a hunter. It has been said that every cat is a beast of prey, even the tame ones. And so it is. The house cat who eats from a bowl or stalks birds in the backyard and the mountain lion who bites through the neck of a deer, have the same instincts. Their physical structure makes them excellent killers.

A natural climber, the mountain lion can spring straight up as high as 18 feet, or drop down 60 feet without getting injured.

◀ UNDERCOVER CATS

Most wild cats that live in dense grass, brush, or jungle have coats that blend with their surroundings. Dappled, spotted, or striped, a cat's coat can make it nearly invisible. Now you see it now you don't—the undercover hunter.

FLEXIBLE FELINES

A cat's spine is so flexible that it can twist and turn and bound at its prey from any angle. This lioness is stretching after having rested most of the day.

SNEAK ATTACK

All good hunters are sneaks, and cats are the sneakiest. Strong muscles allow a cat to stalk and hide, then surprise its prey. With enormous muscle control, this Canadian lynx moves ever so slowly towards its victim, then freezes. A cat can stay motionless for half an hour or more—and then pounce on its startled prey.

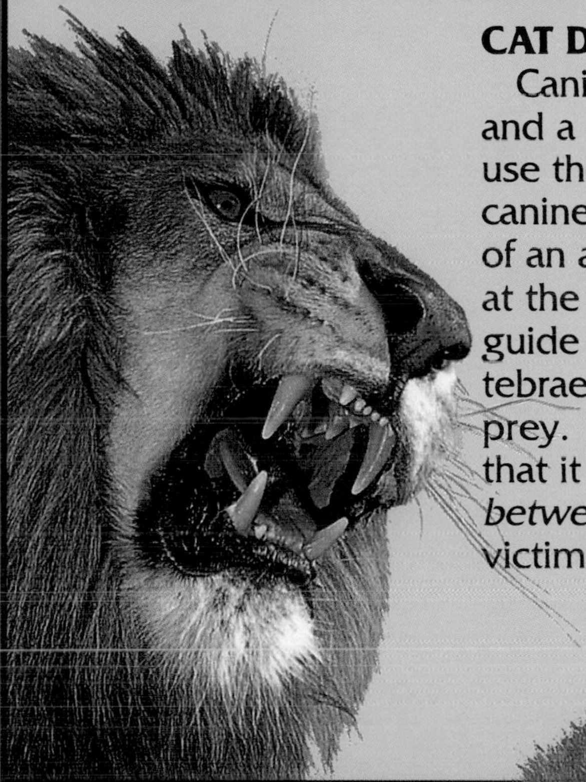

CAT DRACULA

Canine teeth are for killing, and a cat's got the best. Cats use their four dagger-like canine teeth to bite the back of an animal's neck. Nerves at the base of these teeth guide them between the vertebrae (spine bones) of their prey. The bite is so accurate that it cuts the spinal cord *between* the bones and the victim dies instantly.

THE EYES HAVE IT

A cat's eyes are deadly hunting weapons. Their night vision is amazing—six times greater than that of humans. In the dark, the pupils of a cat's eyes expand to take in more light. These pupils, nearly filling the eyes, are strange and beautiful. But beauty is not the point. Detecting prey is the purpose.

PAW CLAWS

Claws are a cat's secret weapon. Most of the time a cat's claws stay inside its paws. During an attack, a cat automatically whips out the claws like razor-edged knives. Afterward, the claws retract to a relaxed position inside the paws. The cat returns to its silent walk, but the claws are always ready.

The outstretched claws of this kitten help it to hang on.

THE LITTLEST CATS

Care to cuddle a lion cub? Is there anything cuter than a kitten? Cats, wild and tame, give birth and care for their offspring in much the same ways. Except for lions, which live in groups, all young cats are cared for by their mother alone. In the wild, cubs lead a dangerous life and must learn to hunt and fend for themselves before leading independent lives.

Lioness and cubs

HOME BODIES▲

All cats are born blind and helpless and feed only on milk for six to eight weeks. But a young cat grows quickly and, in just a week, may double its body weight. A small cat may be on its own in a few months. But the large cats, like the lion and tiger, mature more slowly, and the cubs may depend on their mother for about two years.

AT HOME AND ON THE RANGE

To feed her cubs, a mother cat has to kill at least three times as much prey as when she lives alone. Smaller cats, like this bobcat, bring rodents and other prey back to the den. Larger cats may take their youngsters along and have them practice their hunting skills.

Clouded leopard cub

PLAYING TO KILL▼

Fighting with each other and stalking small animals for fun are the ways young cats learn to hunt on their own. What is playing today is hunting tomorrow. These snow leopard cubs are learning the survival skills they'll need as adults.

This young cheetah is learning, but the unharmed antelope is evidence that the cheetah needs more practice.

GETTING A GRIP

Children may claim that their parents are a pain in the neck, but not cats. Domestic and wild cats carry their young by the back of the neck—with no pain at all. Loose folds of skin on a kitten's neck are a natural handle. But the lion cub (above, left) would rather hitch a ride on its mother's back.

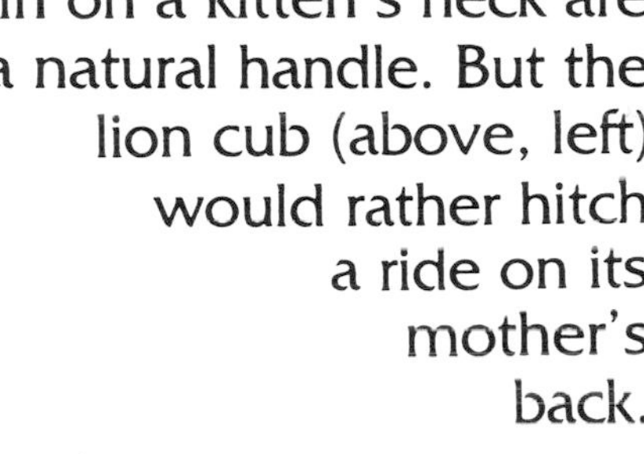

Lynx kitten

CURIOSITY AND THE CAT

All cats are curious, but kittens and cubs are especially anxious to explore their surroundings. Curiosity, however, sometimes gets cats into trouble. This lynx kitten now has to figure out a way to get down.

LEOPARD

CAT UP A TREE

The leopard is the smallest of the big cats, with an average weight of only 100 pounds. A compact powerhouse, the leopard is the master of surprise attack. The most graceful and surefooted of all cats, the leopard is the best tree-climber. Secretive and rarely seen, a leopard can sometimes be spotted by its long, elegant tail dangling from a tree.

LETHAL LEAP

How does a leopard hunt? Patiently and silently. The leopard slinks. It creeps. It belly-crawls ever so carefully towards its prey. Then it *strikes* with a lightning fast leap—graceful, precise, and deadly.

TREETOP DINING

A leopard does not invite guests to dinner. In fact, it often drags its kill up a tree to keep it safe. A leopard can climb a tree with a carcass weighing more than 50 pounds clamped in its jaws. The cat stows the victim over a branch, then takes a good rest knowing that its next meal is close by.

DIFFERENT AND THE SAME

A "black panther" is actually a leopard with a coat of almost invisible black spots on a black background. This beautiful dark cat has a savage reputation. But he is no different from other leopards than a blue-eyed person is from a brown-eyed friend.

THE SOUND OF SILENCE

Do not listen for a leopard. There is not much to hear. The noises a leopard makes are described as a growl or hiss, a rasping yowl or even a cough. It does not roar. Silence seems to suit the leopard best.

◀SPOOKY

The snow leopard looks like the ghost of a leopard. Its thick, woolly coat is a ghostly gray with black spots, well suited for its snowy habitat—the highest, coldest mountains in the world.

LIONS

A MATTER OF PRIDE ▲

Lions are the only cats that live in groups called "prides." As many as 40 cats can live in a pride—several lionesses, their cubs, and one to five adult males. They all live together in a distinct territory, which can extend as far as 10 miles in any direction. The lionesses, which are usually all related, inherit the home range, so they must be especially proud of their pride.

GRRRR!

A lion's roar is so powerful that it can carry for five miles. The great GRRR! is an awesome sound, vibrating like thunder over the plains. Lions roar to stake out their neighborhoods, to let everyone know that the territory is theirs. Their roar is like a huge sign: Keep Off! No Trespassing! Or Else!

LITTLE LIONS

One to five cubs are born in a lion litter, and they depend on their mother for almost two years. Their playtime is their schooltime. They "stalk" each other and "attack" one another, learning the hunting techniques they must know. When they've grown, the females remain at home, but the males are on their own. They set out to search for their own pride.

HUNT CLUB

Lions are the only cats that hunt as a group. They spot prey at a distance and set out with a plan. Surrounding an animal, they drive it toward hidden members waiting to attack. Because they work in groups, lionesses, who do most of the hunting, can easily bring down a wildebeest or zebra and even tackle a giraffe or young elephant—big game even for a big cat.

HUNGRY AS A LION ▼

Lions are not fussy eaters. They eat what they kill, what other predators kill, or animals that just die. And they have no table manners. They snarl and snap at each other, hogging their own portion. They gorge, rather than eat every day. In a single meal, a male lion may eat 80 pounds of meat—and then not eat for a week.

THE KING . . . AND QUEEN . . . OF BEASTS

The lion is known as the King of Beasts for good reason. A male lion can weigh as much as 500 pounds. The female is no less royal at 300. The male, with his magnificent mane, has the look of a monarch. He protects the pride and defends the females against intruders.

SLEEPYHEAD

Lions hunt and eat and. . . sleep. Mostly sleep. It has been said that lions are the laziest animals in Africa. If they've had a good hunt and their bellies are full, lions can spend 18 to 20 hours a day resting or sleeping in the shade.

NUMBER ONE RUNNER

The cheetah is the fastest land animal on earth, for short distances. It streaks across the plains at 70 miles an hour. The cheetah's most important hunting weapon is its amazing, deadly sprint. The cheetah runs for its supper and runs for its life.

CHEETAH

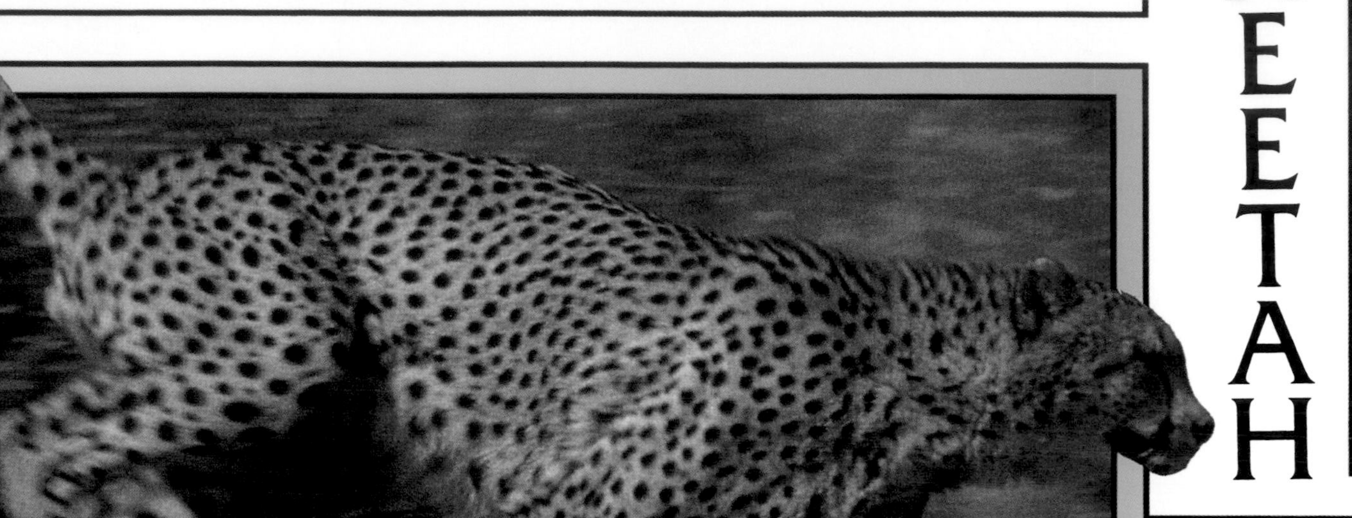

▼ FUNNY FACE

Cheetah cubs are covered with a strange, pale gray fur on their head and back for the first few months. Their faces are funny, too. A cheetah's face is set off by 2 black stripes running from the inner corner of each eye to the mouth. On babies, these lines form an unhappy frown, making cheetah cubs the ugly ducklings of the cat world.

THE ONE AND ONLY

Cheetahs are so unlike other cats that they are a separate species. Their claws do not retract. They do not have powerful jaws. Their canine teeth are not ferocious. They are not strong enough to drag their prey. They cannot roar or climb trees. They do not have long whiskers. They *do* have a deep chest filled with large lungs, and a slender, well-muscled body, built for speed.

ROYAL ROBES▶
The king cheetah wears a royal coat different from the common cheetah. Rare and beautiful, the king has spots that blend into stripes down his back. Having stripes *and* spots makes him a kingly cat indeed.

SPEEDING TO KILL

Faster than a sports car, the cheetah bursts from zero to 40 miles per hour in two seconds. Its claws grip the earth like cleats. Its feet fly, hitting the ground so that, at times, all four feet are airborne. Still running, the cheetah knocks its victim flat, then pounces to kill.

SPRINGY SPINE

The secret to the cheetah's speed is its amazingly flexible spine. When running, the cat arches its back and pulls its feet together. Then, like a spring, its spine uncoils and its legs shoot out, giving the cheetah the longest stride in the cat world.

TIGERS

AWESOME CAT

Mystery, courage, fierceness—these are the characteristics of the biggest cat of them all, the tiger. Five types of tiger roam various parts of Asia. The largest is the Siberian tiger, which can be more than 10 feet long and weigh more than 600 pounds. Rarely seen, the tiger hunts alone at night—a silent, powerful creature, beautiful and frightening.

TIGER TOTS

Tiger cubs are born into a world that can be very hard. They may be killed by other animals while their mother is hunting. At 18 months to two years old, they leave their mother to find their own territory. There they will spend most of their life, hunting and living alone.

BEATING THE HEAT

It's hot in the jungle—steamy and sticky. A tiger can't take its fur coat off, but it can *swim*. Among big cats, the tiger is the most likely to cool off in the water.

Splashing, swimming, lounging up to its neck in lakes and rivers, the tiger knows how to get relief from the heat.

TELLTALE STRIPES

People have fingerprints; tigers have stripes. Every tiger has its own pattern of stripes. Tigers' faces are fierce and beautiful, but they are also unique. A tiger's face markings are so distinctive that they can be used to tell two tigers apart.

SHADOWY FIGURES

The tiger's magnificent striped orange-and-black coat is not just decoration. Stripes are the perfect camouflage in tall grasses and forests, where strips of light filter to the ground through dense leaves. Tigers that live in the northern climates are lighter in color to help them hide in the snow.

PALE FACE

A "white" tiger is not a ghost. It is a genuine tiger with a pink nose and charcoal-colored stripes on a white background. Its eyes may be blue—a tiger of a different hue!

THE STEALTH ATTACK

A tiger is not a hunter that chases prey. It creeps up under cover and gets as close as possible. Then it takes a great leap at the victim and strikes with a lethal weapon—the largest canine teeth of any meat-eating land animal. Still, hunting is not easy. Tigers catch only about one out of every 20 animals they go after.

COUGAR, LYNX, AND BOBCAT

CATS HOT AND COOL

The cougar, lynx, and bobcat are most commonly found in northern climates, but these cats go their separate ways. The lynx is a creature of the snowbound woods. The bobcat prowls most of North America. But the cougar, also known as the puma, the panther, or the mountain lion, is a cat for all climates. It can be found on cold, high peaks, in steaming jungles, in swamplands, and even in deserts.

TUNED IN

A cat with antennae? The lynx has long, glossy, black "tufts" that stick up from each ear. Like hearing aids, they increase the cat's ability to detect the slightest sound. No creak, or snap, or thump in the forest gets by the listening lynx.

▲

DISAPPEARING SPOTS

Adult cougars have sleek, tawny coats that match their spooky yellow eyes. But cougar cubs are spotted with black. At six months, they begin to lose their spots and become cats of one color.

◀This Canadian lynx is marking the pine tree with his scent.

◀A CAT CALLED BOB

A stubby six-inch tail gives the bobcat its name. (To "bob" a tail means to cut it short.) Not a big animal all around, the bobcat weighs about 20 pounds and looks very much like its cousin the lynx.

PHANTOM OF THE FOREST

Bobcats hang out. These cats have favorite places—ledges, tree limbs, and trails—that they come back to again and again. Finding one of these sites may be the only way to lay eyes on a bobcat. These quick-as-a-wink cats are usually seen as fast flashes of fur in the forest.

RACING FOR RABBIT

For mountain cats that live in snow country, the snowshoe hare is a main meal. A swift runner on the biggest rabbit feet around, this hare is still no match for a hungry cat.

KILLER COUGAR

A large male cougar is 200 pounds of muscle. A fierce predator, he can kill a deer with one powerful bite. In his territory, no other animal can challenge him—except a barking dog. The yapping of a poodle sends a cougar up a tree.

CATS WITH A SOUTHERN ACCENT

Cats in Central and South America all test the limits of some feline characteristics. The jaguar has incredible power, the ocelot, extraordinary beauty. The jaguarundi is the most uncatlike creature, and the margay is a gymnast that does tricks in the treetops.

SPOTTED BEAUTY

The ocelot has a coat of many colors. Its background fur runs from reddish brown to cream to white. And its spots are a varied lot: solids, circles, and spots that join together to form stripes. The result is a masterpiece of camouflage and one of the most magnificent coats in the cat world.

A hungry jaguar on the prowl.

Margay

CIRCUS CAT

The margay is a trapeze artist, and its high wire is a tree branch. No bigger than a house cat, the margay scampers around trees like a monkey. An acrobat with special equipment, this cat has ankles that rotate way out and big feet and toes designed for gripping.

Jaguarundi

CAT COUPLES

The jaguarundi looks more like a weasel than a cat. It has a long body with legs that seem too short and a head that appears too small. But the jaguarundi male and female find each other attractive and, unlike most other cats, they live together for long periods of time.

ONE FIERCE CAT

Caimans and turtles beware! Monkeys, too! The jaguar plunges into rivers and scrambles up trees to feed its appetite. It dives; it swims; it leaps tall trees with a single bound. When this meat-eater is hungry, no one is safe!

WEATHERMAN

The jaguar is at home just about everywhere — mountains, grasslands, and rain forests. Everywhere it goes, the jaguar proclaims its presence with a roar that makes mountains tremble, grasses shiver, and jungles quiver. Amazon Indians still believe that the roar of the jaguar is the sound of thunder that announces approaching rain.

UNCOMMON CATS

Cats are exotic creatures, magnificent and mysterious, but also strange, and even bizarre. The cat kingdom has some surprising, remarkable, and fascinating felines.

RABBIT EARS ▼

The serval's head is smaller than the body. It has big ears that look more like they belong on a rabbit than a cat. But these ears serve the serval well. It can hear small animals hidden in grasses and pounce as quick as a...rabbit.

MOST WANTED

Geoffrey's cat has a distinction no other cat wants. Its fur is the most traded pelt in the world. Prized for its beauty, its exotic coat has black spots and colors ranging from smokey-gray to tawny yellow.

◀ SLAM DUNK

The caracal can leap into the air and swat a bird to the ground like a basketball player dunking a ball into the net. Its nickname is the "desert lynx" because it lives in dry areas and its ear tufts are similar to those of the lynx.

TAMING THE WILD ▶

The jungle cat is a wild cat known to raid chicken coops. This does not make it a welcome guest in the villages near its habitat. But the jungle cat's kittens can be easily tamed—a reminder that with some cats, at least, the difference between wild and tame can be a fine line.

▲ AQUA CAT

The fishing cat gets its name, of course, from fishing. This cat sits by the water and waits. If a fish comes by, it raises a paw and flips the unsuspecting prey onto the land and eats it. The fishing cat has webbed feet like a duck so it can swim better and hunt where most other cats will not bother —in the water.

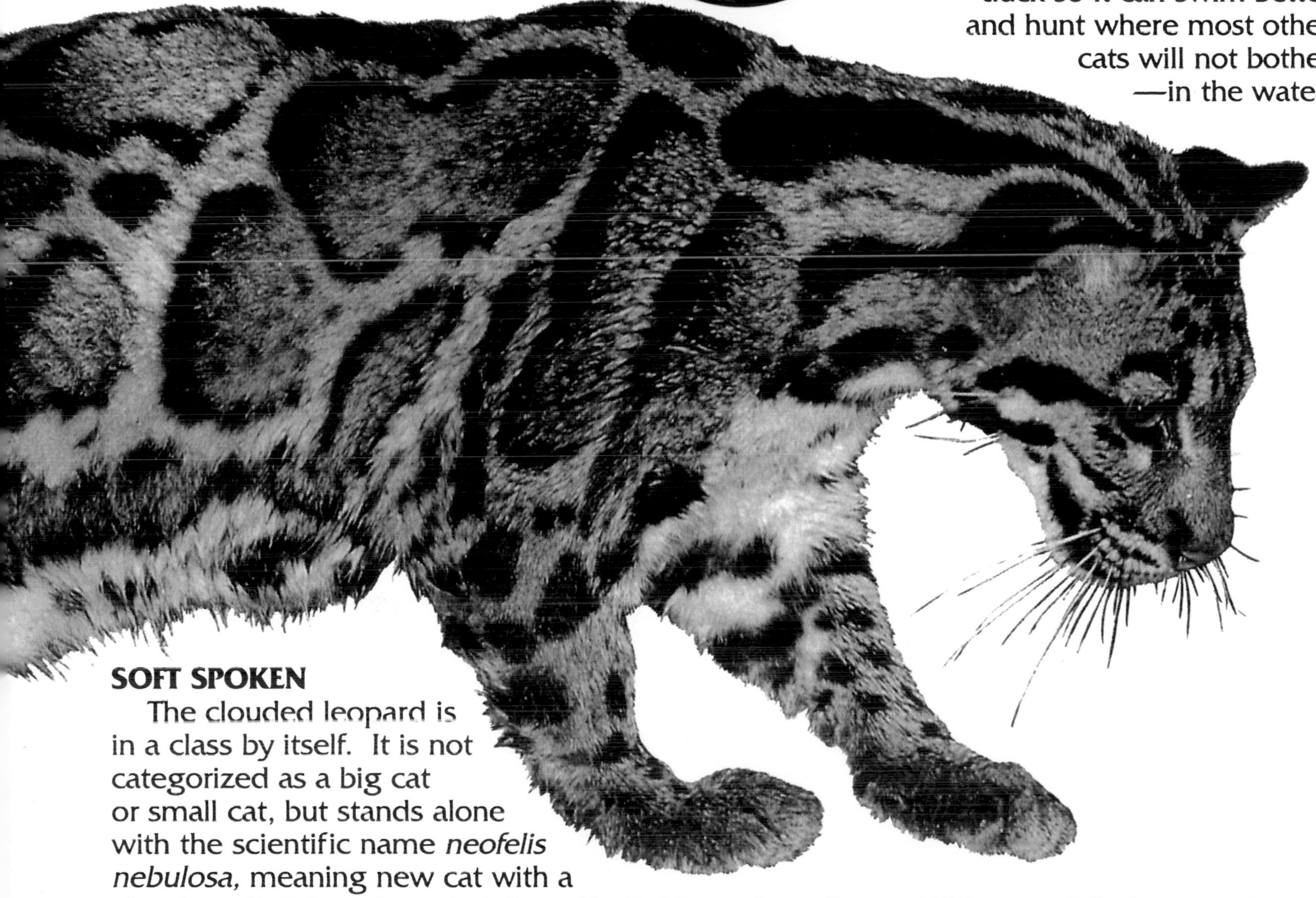

SOFT SPOKEN

The clouded leopard is in a class by itself. It is not categorized as a big cat or small cat, but stands alone with the scientific name *neofelis nebulosa,* meaning new cat with a cloudy pelt. It has characteristics of both big and small cats. With especially long canine teeth, this cat has a fierce look but cannot roar. The clouded leopard is a purring cat.

BEES AND WASPS

Most people will probably live their whole lives without coming face to face with a lion, python, or Komodo dragon. But bees and wasps are a part of everyday life nearly anywhere you live. They are very dangerous, and for many people they are the scariest.

◀ HAIL THE QUEEN

A queen bee's main function as a member of the colony is to reproduce. A well-mated and well-fed queen bee of the colony can lay about 2,000 eggs a day! That's more than a queen bee's own bodyweight. A queen bee is surrounded by worker bees who give her food and dispose of her waste.

COLONY LIVING ▼

Most bees and wasps live in large groups called colonies. Colony life revolves around serving the queen. Workers or drones gather nectar from flowers, build the nests, and fiercely defend their queen. If a person gets too close to a beehive or wasps' nest, the workers fly into action to protect their queen. This is when dangerous swarm attacks can occur. As with any dangerous animal, it is always best to bee-careful!

◀ ALLERGIC REACTIONS

Bees such as honeybees can be really dangerous to people who are allergic, especially if they receive a large number of stings from a fallen beehive. The sting toxin quickly attacks the person's immune system, and in extreme cases can result in death.

PAINFUL STINGS ▶

Their stings are painful, but usually a single sting is not life threatening. The danger comes when bees or wasps attack in swarms. When hundreds or thousands of these flying insects sting a person within a few seconds, the attack can kill. Deadly attacks like these are rare. They usually happen when people disturb the insects' home.

CUCKOO BUMBLEBEES ▼

One species of bumblebee, called the cuckoo bumblebee, has lost the ability to collect pollen. A female cuckoo will sneak into another bumblebee colony, and after subduing the queen bee, will force the worker bees to feed her and her offspring.

◀ WASP WITH VENOM

Wasps can paralyze their prey by injecting it with venom. Their stinger is also their egg-laying device. One of the differences between wasps and bees is that wasps use venom designed to paralyze prey, and bees use venom that causes pain.

BEARS

These amazing creatures are some of the largest land animals on earth. One of nature's wildest wonders, bears swim, climb, run at surprisingly high speeds, and travel great distances in one day.

This fun-loving ▶ grizzly enjoys a roll in a field of berries.

WALKING UPRIGHT ▼

A bear usually walks on all fours. But a curious bear will stand up on its back legs to get a better view or to pull down food from above. To defend itself, a bear will rear up and lash out with its massive paws.

NOT TOO CLOSE

People like to think of bears as cute and cuddly. But bears like to stay far away from people. If startled or provoked, a bear may even attack.

◀ BIG DIET

Bears are big eaters. They are classified as *carnivores,* or meat-eaters, but all have a diet that includes plants. They may also dine on honey, mushrooms, and many other things.

▶ Through bear talk, cubs learn from their mother.

▼ Brown bears roar when they're really angry.

NOT A BEAR

The Australian koala bear is not a member of the bear family at all. A marsupial like the kangaroo, the koala carries and nurses its young in a stomach pouch.

CHATTER ▲

Although they are fairly quiet, bears do communicate with sound. They growl when threatened and hum when content. They even whine and cry when they're upset.

LIVING ALONE

Bears rule wherever they live. Their only enemies, besides people, are other bears. Solitary creatures, they usually avoid one another. Only when it's time to mate do adult males and females get together. A mother bear, however, may spend a couple of years with her cubs.

BEAR COUNTRY

Ever wonder if there are bears living nearby? They might be! Bears can be found on all continents except Africa, Antarctica, and Australia. There are eight living species, which come in a variety of colors.

BROWN BEAR

Found in Europe, in Asia as far south as India, in western Canada, Alaska, and parts of the western United States, brown bears have the greatest range of all. They are also some of the largest bears, weighing over 800 pounds on average and measuring up to 10 feet from nose to tail.

BLACK BEAR

The tree-climbing black bear inhabits forests, swamps, and wooded mountains from Alaska and Canada down to Mexico and Florida.

ASIATIC BLACK BEAR

The Asiatic black bear lives in brushlands and forests throughout Asia, including Japan and the island of Taiwan.

POLAR BEAR

As wintry white as the ice and snow of the North Pole, the polar bear inhabits Arctic areas in Norway, Greenland, Russia, Canada, and Alaska.

SLOTH BEAR

The sloth bear lives throughout the Indian subcontinent, from Nepal and Bhutan down to Sri Lanka. A fairly small bear, it has a white or yellow "necklace" on its black chest.

SPECTACLED BEAR

There's only one bear that lives in South America, and that's the spectacled bear. This unique creature, which gets its name from the markings around its eyes, roams along the Andes Mountains in Venezuela, Colombia, Ecuador, Peru, and Bolivia.

SUN BEAR

Smallest of all the bears, the sun bear averages 100 pounds and measures about four feet long. It keeps to the dense Southeast Asian forests of Sumatra, Borneo, the Malayan Peninsula, Myanmar, and Thailand.

GIANT PANDA

The giant panda makes its home in the high mountains of central China, where bamboo, its favorite food, is plentiful. The rare panda is confined to an area only 300 miles long and about 80 miles wide.

BIG BODIES

How would you describe a bear? Look carefully. Most bears have a large head with a long snout, small close-set eyes, and erect ears. Their heavily built body has short, thick limbs and a stumpy tail. And, yes, they are big and furry!

Talk about big! There once was a polar bear that weighed over 2,000 pounds and measured 11 feet long.

FANTASTIC FUR

Fairly uniform in color, bear fur can be either black, white, or many shades of brown. But several species have light-colored markings on their chest that accent their size when they rear up to fight or defend themselves.

▲ GRIN AND BEAR IT

Most bears have 42 teeth. Their sharp canines can tear flesh from a carcass, while their broad, flat molars allow them to grind down plants.

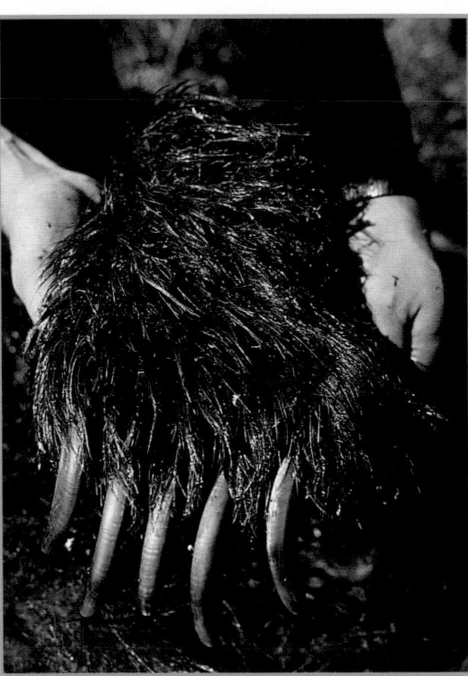

Unlike the claws of most cats, a bear's claws can't be pulled in when not in use.

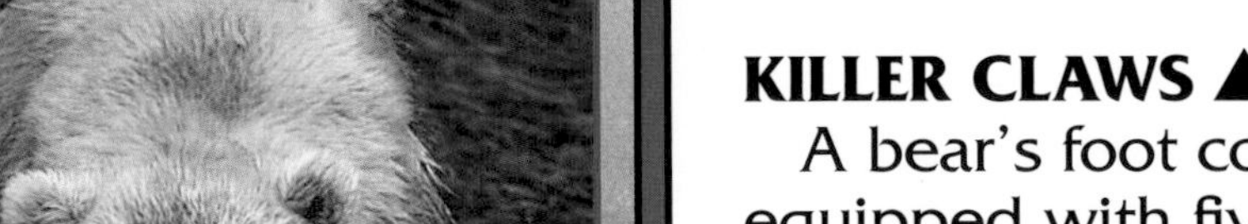

KILLER CLAWS ▲

A bear's foot comes equipped with five long, curved claws. Bears use these sharp, all-purpose claws to mark or climb trees, dig for food, excavate their dens, rip apart prey, scratch, or defend themselves.

NEARSIGHTED ▶

Bears are built for seeing small things close at hand, such as berries and other food. In fact, they are fairly nearsighted and sometimes get so absorbed in eating that they don't see an approaching person. Hikers often whistle or wear bells to alert bears of their presence.

◀ BODY LANGUAGE

Bears not only use their body for movement, but also to communicate. A stare from a bear is a serious threat. But when a bear lowers its head, that means it wants peace. Bears also mark trees or other objects in their territory with their scent or claw marks.

NOSING AROUND

Smell is probably a bear's greatest sense. Like a bloodhound, it can accurately sniff out a trail where prey walked many hours before. It can also pick up a scent from the air and find the source miles and miles away.

FAST FEET

They may look slow and clumsy, but bears walk like people—on the soles of their feet, with heels touching the ground. Some are also fast runners. Brown bears can reach speeds of up to 40 miles per hour—faster than any Olympian sprinter and as fast as a greyhound!

STAYING COOL ▶

During the summer, bears have to stay cool, especially polar bears, which are built for very cold weather. They spread out and expose their massive body to the air or ice.

▶This sleepy polar bear cools itself off in some Arctic slush.

LEAVING THE DEN

When spring arrives, bears leave their den to search for food. During their first weeks outside, when the only available food may be grasses, herbs, and twigs, bears tend to lose weight. Adults also shed their thick coats so they'll be cooler in the summer months ahead.

In Alaska, ▶ this bear is enjoying a meal of blueberries.

HARVEST TIME

In the forest, as new foods ripen in late summer, the bear family gorges on berries, fruits, and nuts. They spend more and more time eating, storing up a thick layer of fat to provide energy and extra insulation during the long winter months.

The fruit of a rose, called ▶ a rose hip, is a tasty treat for a grizzly bear cub.

FINDING A MATE

For several months in the spring, bears leave their solitary habits behind to seek out a mate. Courtship may include vicious fights among competing males. Mating bears sometimes spend a few days together, but the males soon leave to seek out another female.

These two male grizzly bears are preparing to fight.

TO THE DEN

In the fall, bears begin their task of homemaking. Female polar bears dig their winter home in snowbanks. The Asiatic black bear makes a bed of fresh twigs on the forest floor. Grizzlies dig out homes underground, chewing off branches to build springy mattresses. Black bears find a denning space in a cave.

◀ A black bear mother and cub cuddle up in their den.

A black bear mother ▶ nursing her two little cubs.

READY FOR SLEEP

When a bear enters its winter den, it is fat, has a thick coat, and is ready for sleep. Body temperature lowers and heart rate decreases. Cubs that spend more than one season with their mother accompany her into the den, but otherwise a bear sleeps alone.

WINTER BABIES

Cubs are born during the winter in the shelter of a den. Very tiny at birth, the cubs spend the first weeks of their lives nursing and sleeping.

Polar bear cubs snuggle ▶ into the warmth of their mother's fur.

EATING EVERYTHING

Bears are omnivorous—they will gobble down just about anything in sight. And that may be the secret to their success—they are not fussy eaters and can find a tasty meal just about anywhere.

▼ Not great hunters, black bears eat mostly plant matter, including grass, berries, acorns, roots, and herbs.

A SEASONAL DIET

A bear's diet may change from season to season—the tender roots or shoots of spring plants, ripe summer berries and fruit, and acorns in the fall. In the spring, bears also eat trees, peeling away the bark to get at the inner layer, called *cambium.*

EATING MEAT

Bears are not the great killers many people think they are. They do catch and eat small animals, and some, like the polar bear, eat more meat than others. But when it comes to eating larger prey, bears mostly feed on animals that are already dead.

◀ On the coast of Alaska, this hungry grizzly attacks a razor clam.

FISHING

Alaskan brown bears are great at fishing. They grab fish in their mouth or pin them down with their front paws. They even leap from overhanging boulders and plunge into the water to nab a passing fish. Gathering at streams and rivers during the salmon run, brown bears may eat as much as 90 pounds of fish in one day!

▼ PATIENT HUNTER

The predatory polar bear has several hunting techniques. In one, called "still hunting," the bear sniffs out a seal's "breathing hole" and then may wait patiently for hours above it. When a seal surfaces for air, the bear instantly delivers a powerful blow, grabs with its sharp, pointed teeth, and hauls it out of the water.

▼ UNHAPPY CAMPERS

When a bear is around, nothing edible is safe. Campers come out of their tents in the morning to find packages of food ripped open, jars smashed, and coolers overturned. The best remedy is to buy "bear-proof" containers or hang the food out of reach.

IN THE DUMPS

Garbage dumps are an open invitation to hungry bears. As the bears lose their fear of people and become more dependent upon them for food, they may actually become more dangerous.

FOUR LITTLE BEARS

Take a look at the spectacled, sun, sloth, and Asiatic bears. They're the smallest of all bears, and they are very unique.

◀ A mother sun bear and her cub.

SUN BEAR

The sun bear is the smallest of the bears—about three to four-and-a-half feet long and 100 pounds. Some people try to make this little black bear a pet, only to discover later that it's uncontrollable. The sun bear is one of the most dangerous animals in its territory.

TROUBLEMAKER ▲

Of all the bears, the Asiatic black is most likely to make trouble with people living in its territory. It has been known to raid herds of cattle, sheep, and goats, and to destroy crops. It also has a reputation for being ill-tempered and has attacked people.

▼ A sun bear snoozing in a tree.

FRUIT LOVER ▶

If there's one thing the South American spectacled bear loves, it's fruit. After building a platform from branches high in a fruit-laden tree, it will settle in for days of feasting. When it has eaten all the fruit within reach, it picks up and moves to a new site.

▼ The spectacled bear.

LIVING VACUUM ▼

The sloth bear loves termites, its staple food. To get at them, it digs a hole in the nest, sticks its muzzle in, and blows violently to clean the surrounding area. Closing its nostrils, it then sucks in the insects. The sounds a sloth bear makes while vacuuming up its meal can be heard 200 yards away!

When playfighting, ▶ sloth bears can look pretty fierce. But unlike most bears, they actually like the company.

◀ TOP OF THE CLASS

Captive sun bears have proven their intelligence in amazing ways. One young bear figured out how to use its huge, curved claw as a key, unlocking a cupboard and taking out a sugarbowl. Another scattered rice from its dish to attract chickens, which it then killed and ate.

NORTHERN GIANTS

Amidst the ice floes of the Arctic Circle lives the polar bear—the king of the north. This bear reaches gigantic sizes, and does so by eating meat. A skilled hunter, the polar bear has been known to attack beluga whales, jumping on their back, then riding them under the sea.

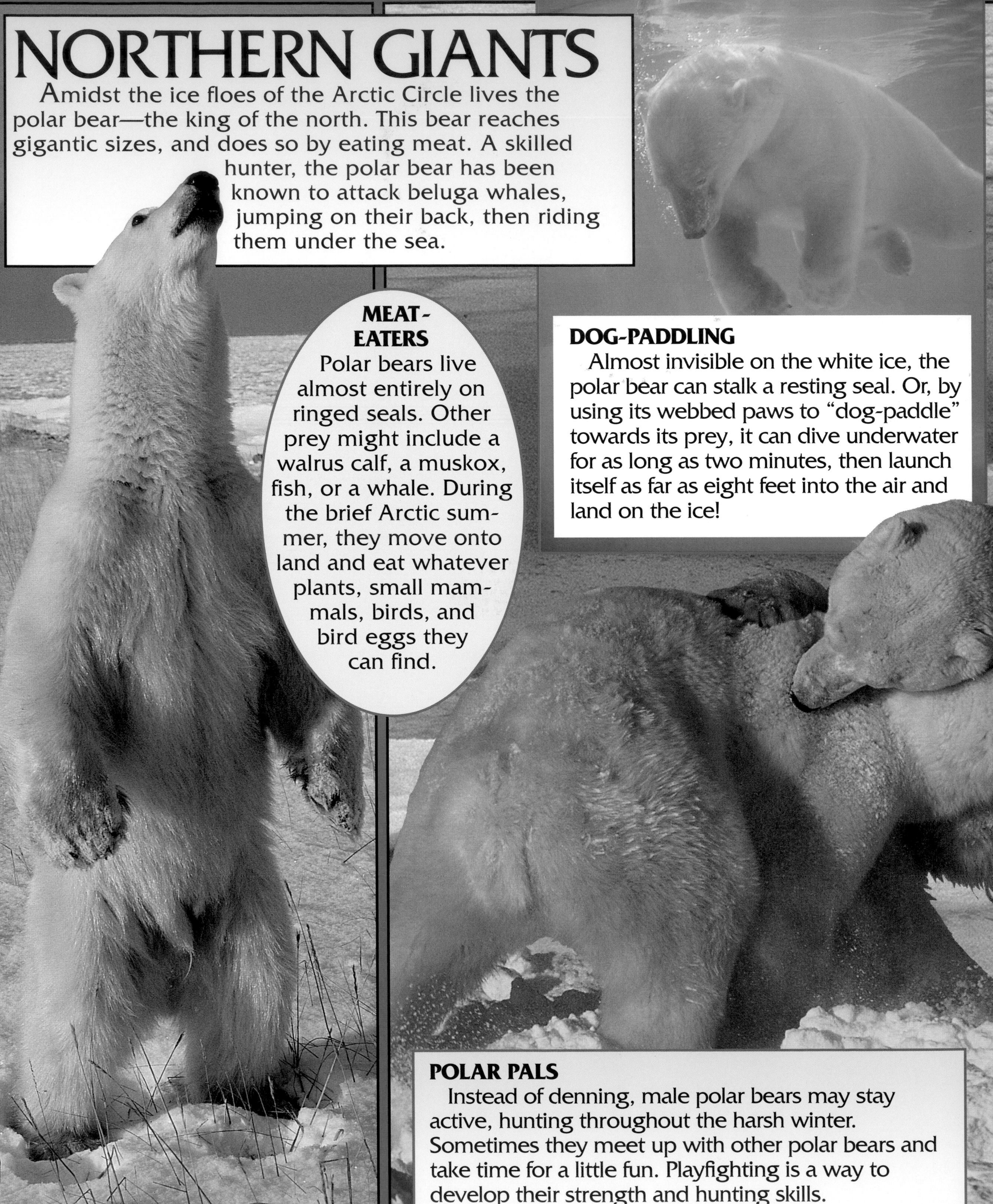

MEAT-EATERS

Polar bears live almost entirely on ringed seals. Other prey might include a walrus calf, a muskox, fish, or a whale. During the brief Arctic summer, they move onto land and eat whatever plants, small mammals, birds, and bird eggs they can find.

DOG-PADDLING

Almost invisible on the white ice, the polar bear can stalk a resting seal. Or, by using its webbed paws to "dog-paddle" towards its prey, it can dive underwater for as long as two minutes, then launch itself as far as eight feet into the air and land on the ice!

POLAR PALS

Instead of denning, male polar bears may stay active, hunting throughout the harsh winter. Sometimes they meet up with other polar bears and take time for a little fun. Playfighting is a way to develop their strength and hunting skills.

CURIOUS COAT

Perfectly insulated, the polar bear has a thick layer of fat under its skin and more fur than any other bear. Fur on the soles of its paws helps the bear grip ice. Surprisingly, polar bear fur is hollow. The hair collects light from the sun and channels the heat to the polar bear's black skin. Because the skin is black, it absorbs the heat.

A nap is a good way for polar bears to conserve energy in the cold Arctic.

SNOWY DENS

In the fall, females start digging their winter dens in the snowbanks. Warm air gets trapped inside, and drifting snow covers the opening. In late December or early January the female gives birth, usually to twins.

This polar bear cub stays warm inside its den.

MOM KNOWS BEST

When the polar bear family breaks out of the den in March or April, the cubs weigh about 22 pounds and have thick fur coats. For nearly two years they watch their mother closely, learning the hunting skills needed for survival.

ALL-AMERICAN

With its powerful body, the North American black bear can outrun a person, shinny up a tree with amazing speed, and easily break through dense underbrush in a forest. Although called a black bear, it comes in many colors, such as blue-black, brown, cinnamon, or even white.

▼ A cinnamon-colored black bear.

SIZING UP

An adult male black bear is about 4 to 6 feet long when fully grown and can weigh up to about 580 pounds. As with most bear species, males are considerably larger than females.

CURLING UP ▼

Black bears usually curl up for the winter in a cave. Some of them will dig a den under the roots of a large tree. If the trees have been logged out, they make beds on the ground amongst thick vegetation, raking up leaves and plants to lie on.

GHOST BEAR

Found only in a small area of British Columbia, Canada, the Kermode bear is the white version of a black bear. Also called "ghost bears," Kermode bears are so rare that few people have actually seen them.

◀ UP A TREE

When a black bear cub leaves the den, its claws are already well developed. The cub needs them, because every time the mother bear senses danger, she will chase her cubs into the nearest tree.

A black bear mother ▶ and her cub.

BARE SOLES

Bears that stay on the ground most of the time, like polar bears, have feet with hairy soles. But black bears, which spend much of their life in trees, have bare soles. Along with sharp, narrow, curved claws, bare soles make it easier for the black bear to climb.

MIXED MENU ▶

The black bear is a powerful swimmer and good fisher. On land, the bear flips over stones and decayed logs to find insects and grubs. It digs out burrows to reach small rodents. It also feeds on vegetation, such as berries, and loves honey.

A black bear taking a swim.

MIGHTY BEAR

Along with polar bears, brown bears rank as the largest of all bears. The heaviest yet recorded weighed more than 2,000 pounds. Perhaps the best-known brown bear is the mighty grizzly. "Grizzled" means partly gray, which perfectly describes the gray-tipped hairs of a grizzly's shaggy coat.

THE BROWN FAMILY

One of the largest brown bears is the Kodiak, found only on Kodiak Island in southern Alaska. Other brown bears include the Siberian bear, the red bear of northern India and the Himalayas, the Manchurian bear, the horse bear of Tibet and western China, and the Hokkaido bear of Japan.

TOP BEAR ▲

Spectacular fights occur between big, male brown bears when they are courting and when they gather at rivers to fish for migrating salmon. If the challenged bear does not turn his head and back up, the two go at each other with vicious lunges, slapping and biting until one bear gives up.

◀ HUMPBACK

Ranging in color from light cream to black, brown bears are sometimes confused with black bears. However, brown bears are larger, have round faces, and have a hump on their back. The hump is a mass of muscles that gives them added power for digging and fighting.

EVERY BITE
Grizzlies eat everything, including fungi, leaves, berries, roots, sprouting plants, insects, fish, and small mammals. When they find the carcasses of larger animals, like moose, elk, or livestock, they store the remains, returning again and again to the storage site until every last morsel is consumed.

AMAZING CLAWS
Grizzlies and other brown bears have enormous claws, which sometimes reach six inches in length. With these tools they do battle, dig, climb, handle food, and scratch. One very skilled grizzly was even seen handling a feather, turning it over and over in its paws.

▲ CUB-SITTING
Grizzlies are not as solitary as was once thought. Female grizzlies will adopt motherless cubs and may even develop friendships. In the McNeil River area of Alaska, two females met one another almost every day and swapped cubs over an entire summer.

Photo Credits

- Dreamstime: Cover
- Fotolia: Cover; End Pages (Front)
- iStock: Cover; pages 26-27, 33, 54, 56-57
- Creatas/North American Wildlife: End Pages (Front); pages 2-3
- PhotoDisc/Nature, Wildlife and the Environment 2: End Pages (Back)
- Mark Picard/NE Stock Photo: page 4
- A. Kerstitch/Visuals Unlimited: page 4
- Joe McDonald/Visuals Unlimited: pages 4, 69, 75
- J. H. Robinson/Photo Researchers: page 5
- Nathan W. Cohen/Visuals Unlimited: pages 6-7
- Jim Merli/Visuals Unlimited: page 6
- Lawrence E. Naylor/Photo Researchers: page 7
- Tom McHugh/Photo Researchers: pages 7, 29
- Creatas: pages 8-9,
- IT Stock Free/Creatas: pages 8-9, 32-33
- Zig Leszczynski: pages 9, 61, 65, 68, 75
- R.E. Barber: pages 9, 11, 17, 19, 37, 45, 51
- Kit Breen: page 12
- Alan & Sandy Carey: pages 14, 20
- Tom & Pat Leeson: pages 10-12, 14-16, 19, 22, 58-61, 64, 66-69, 72-75
- John & Ann Mahan: pages 12-13, 18, 20
- Rick McIntyre: pages 15, 18
- Lynn Rogers: pages 12, 18
- Thomas Kitchin/First Light: pages 10, 19
- Peter McLeod/First Light: pages 11-12, 14, 16, 20-21
- Jim Zuckerman/First Light: page 13
- Robert Lankinen/Wildlife Collection: pages 21, 70-71
- Michael Evan Sewell/Visual Pursuit: page 22
- Michael Francis/Wildlife Collection: pages 11, 23, 58
- Doug Perrine/DRK: pages 24-25
- Amos Nachoum/Innerspace Visions: page 24
- Stephen Frink/WaterHouse: page 25
- Ron & Valerie Taylor/WaterHouse: page 25
- Norbert Wu: page 25
- Carl Roessler/DigitalVision: page 27
- Paul E. Clark/NE Stock Photo: page 28
- Walt Anderson/Visuals Unlimited: page 28
- W. A. Banaszewski/Visuals Unlimited: page 32
- Thomas C. Boyden: page 32
- Jeffrey W. Lang/Photo Researchers: page 33
- Tom J. Ulrich/Visuals Unlimited: page 33
- Larry Ulrich/DRK: page 32
- Erwin & Peggy Bauer: pages 36, 38, 40-42, 44, 46-47, 49-51, 53-54
- Norvia Behling: pages 38, 54
- Tony La Gruth: page 48
- James Martin: pages 50, 55
- Laura Riley: pages 37, 39
- Kevin Schafer: pages 48, 52-53
- Rita Summers: pages 34, 36, 42, 50
- Charles Summers: pages 41, 44
- Robert Winslow: pages 34, 38-39, 41, 50-51
- Samburu G.R./Animals Animals: page 43
- Gerard Lacz/Animals Animals: page 61
- Tim Davis/Davis-Lynn Photography: pages 34-39, 42, 42, 48-49, 52
- Renee Lynn/Davis-Lynn Photography: pages 34-36, 41-42, 44-46
- John Giustina/Wildlife Collection: pages 37, 46, 58, 69
- Martin Harvey/Wildlife Collection: pages 36, 40, 42, 60
- Dean Lee/Wildlife Collection: page 45
- Ron Maratea/International Stock Photos: page 49
- Digital Vision/Creatas: pages 56-57
- Breck P. Kent: pages 58, 62
- Lynn M. Stone: page 74
- Fred Bruemmer/DRK: page 63
- Johnny Johnson/DRK: pages 58, 62, 60-61, 70-71
- Stephen J. Krasemann/DRK: pages 63, 67
- Wayne Lynch/DRK: pages 58-59, 61, 62, 68, 71-72
- Belinda Wright/DRK: page 60
- Mark Newman/International Stock: pages 69-71
- Will Regan/International Stock: page 67
- Tom Edwards/Visuals Unlimited: page 59
- Ken Lucas/Visuals Unlimited: page 62
- William J. Weber/Visuals Unlimited: page 60
- Gary Schultz/Wildlife Collection: pages 59, 73
- Jack Swenson/Wildlife Collection: page 66
- Tom Vezo/Wildlife Collection: page 66

- Illustration:
- Crystal Palette: page 5